PRENTICE HALL
WORLD STUDIES
WESTERN HEMISPHERE

Reading and Vocabulary Study Guide

PEARSON

Prentice
Hall

Boston, Massachusetts
Upper Saddle River, New Jersey

The maps on pages 3, 11, and 165 are based on maps created by **DK Cartography**.

Prentice Hall® and Pearson Prentice Hall™ are trademarks, in the U.S. and/or in other countries, of Pearson Education, Inc., or its affiliate(s).

0-13-251636-5

3 4 5 6 7 8 9 10   11 10 09 08

Table of Contents

How to Use This Book

The Reading and Vocabulary Study Guide was designed to help you understand World Studies content. It will also help you build your reading and vocabulary skills. Please take the time to look at the next few pages to see how it works!

The Prepare to Read page gets you ready to read each section.

Objectives from your textbook help you focus your reading.

With each chapter, you will study a Target Reading Skill. This skill is introduced in your textbook, but explained more here. Later, questions or activities in the margin will help you practice the skill.

You are given a new Vocabulary Strategy with each chapter. Questions or activities in the margin later will help you practice the strategy.

CHAPTER 1

Prepare to Read

Section 2 Climate and Vegetation

Objectives

1. Find out what kinds of climate Latin America has.
2. Learn what factors influence climate in Latin America.
3. Understand how climate and vegetation influence the ways people live.

Target Reading Skill

Preview and Predict Before you read, make a prediction or a guess about what you will be learning. Predicting is another way to set a purpose for reading. It will help you remember what you read. Follow these steps: (1) Preview the section title, objectives, headings, and table on the pages in Section 2. (2) Predict something you might learn about Latin America. Based on your preview, you will probably predict that you will learn more about Latin America's climate and plants.

List two facts that you predict you will learn about Latin America's climate and plants.

_____

_____

As you read, check your predictions. How correct were they? If they were not very accurate, try to pay closer attention when you preview.

Vocabulary Strategy

Using Context Clues to Determine Meaning You will probably come across words you haven't seen before when you read. Sometimes you can pick up clues about the meaning of an unfamiliar word by reading the words, phrases, and sentences that surround it. The underlined words in the sentences below give clues to the meaning of the word *dense*.

The Amazon rain forest is *dense* with plants and trees. The plant life is <u>so crowded</u> that almost <u>no sunlight reaches the ground</u>.

Unfamiliar Word	Clues	Meaning
dense	so crowded no sunlight	thick, close together crowded

Section Summary pages provide an easy-to-read summary of each section.

Provides a summary of the section's most important ideas.

Large blue headings correspond to large red headings in your textbook.

This checkmark tells you when to answer the Reading Check question.

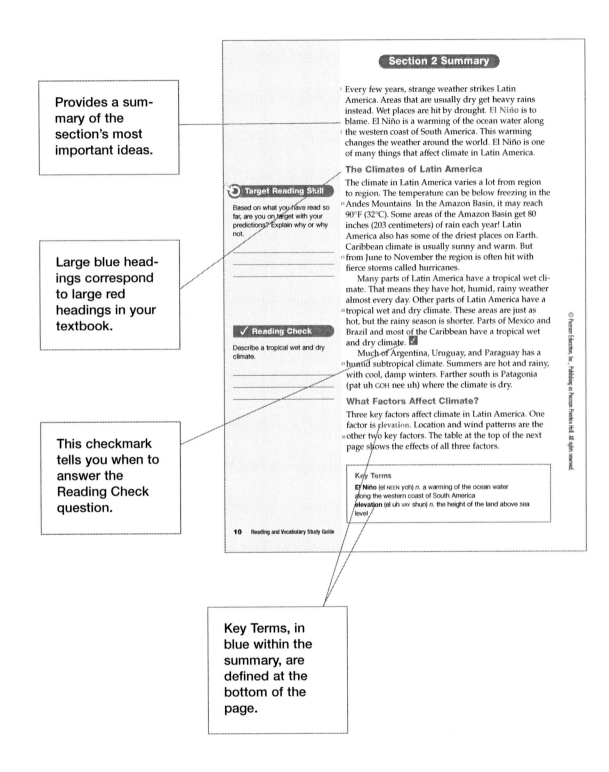

Section 2 Summary

Every few years, strange weather strikes Latin America. Areas that are usually dry get heavy rains instead. Wet places are hit by drought. El Niño is to blame. El Niño is a warming of the ocean water along the western coast of South America. This warming changes the weather around the world. El Niño is one of many things that affect climate in Latin America.

The Climates of Latin America

The climate in Latin America varies a lot from region to region. The temperature can be below freezing in the Andes Mountains. In the Amazon Basin, it may reach 90°F (32°C). Some areas of the Amazon Basin get 80 inches (203 centimeters) of rain each year! Latin America also has some of the driest places on Earth. Caribbean climate is usually sunny and warm. But from June to November the region is often hit with fierce storms called hurricanes.

Many parts of Latin America have a tropical wet climate. That means they have hot, humid, rainy weather almost every day. Other parts of Latin America have a tropical wet and dry climate. These areas are just as hot, but the rainy season is shorter. Parts of Mexico and Brazil and most of the Caribbean have a tropical wet and dry climate.

Much of Argentina, Uruguay, and Paraguay has a humid subtropical climate. Summers are hot and rainy, with cool, damp winters. Farther south is Patagonia (pat uh GOH nee uh) where the climate is dry.

What Factors Affect Climate?

Three key factors affect climate in Latin America. One factor is elevation. Location and wind patterns are the other two key factors. The table at the top of the next page shows the effects of all three factors.

Target Reading Skill

Based on what you have read so far, are you on target with your predictions? Explain why or why not.

_____

_____

_____

✓ Reading Check

Describe a tropical wet and dry climate.

_____

_____

_____

Key Terms

El Niño (el NEEN yoh) *n.* a warming of the ocean water along the western coast of South America
elevation (el uh VAY shun) *n.* the height of the land above sea level

Key Terms, in blue within the summary, are defined at the bottom of the page.

Questions and activities in the margin help you take notes on main ideas, and practice the Target Reading Skill and Vocabulary Strategy.

Causes	Effects
Elevation	The higher the elevation, the colder the temperature
Location	Regions close to the Equator are warmer than those farther away ☑
Wind patterns	Sea breezes keep temperatures mild and bring more rain

Climate, Plants, and People

The Amazon rain forest is dense with thousands of types of plants. The air is hot and moist. In contrast, the Atacama (ah tah KAH mah) Desert in Chile has few
35 signs of life because it is very dry. Latin America's physical features make such climate extremes possible.

Many regions of Latin America have less extreme climates. <u>They have different kinds of vegetation, or plant life.</u> Temperature and rainfall affect what plants
40 grow in a region. They also affect what crops people can grow. For example, sugar cane, coffee, and bananas need warm weather and much rain. These three crops are important in Latin America. The economy of many countries depends on exporting these crops.
45 Elevation also affects vegetation. The higher the elevation, the cooler and drier it is. Plants must be able to survive in these conditions. ☑

Review Questions

1. What are four climates common in Latin America?

_____

_____

2. How does climate affect the people and the economy of Latin America?

_____

_____

Key Term

economy (ih KAHN uh mee) *n.* the ways that goods and services are made and brought to people

✓ Reading Check

How does being near to the Equator affect climate?

_____

_____

_____

Vocabulary Strategy

Look at the word *vegetation* in the underlined sentence. Underline the surrounding words or phrases that are clues to the word's meaning.

✓ Reading Check

Describe how elevation affects the vegetation of a region.

_____

_____

_____

Use write-on lines to answer the questions. You can also use the lines to take notes.

When you see this symbol, mark the text as indicated.

Questions at the end of each section and chapter help you review content and assess your own understanding.

Chapter 1 Assessment

...ree geographic regions of Latin America are
...exico, Brazil, and Peru.
...e Amazon, the Andes, and the Río de la Plata system.
...iddle America, the Caribbean, and South America.
...ral, isthmus, and tributary.

...mazon River is
...exico's greatest resource.
...e cause of hurricanes in the Caribbean each year.
...xt to the Andes Mountains in Chile.
...e of the largest rivers in the world.

...hid subtropical climate is
  A. one in which the weather is hot and rainy all year round.
  B. hot, but the rainy season lasts only part of the year.
  C. similar to the climate in parts of the southern United States.
  D. found in the area called Patagonia.

4. Climate in Latin America is influenced by nearness to the Equator,
  A. vegetation, and the economy.
  B. elevation, and wind patterns.
  C. location, and wind speed.
  D. rivers, and deserts.

5. The amount of natural resources in Latin America can best be described as
  A. the same throughout the region.
  B. similar to that of the United States.
  C. a sign of the region's economic diversity.
  D. uneven from country to country.

Short Answer Question

How does the physical geography of Latin America affect the people who live there?

_____

_____

_____

_____

Foundations of Geography

Objectives

1. Learn about the study of Earth.
2. Discover five ways to look at Earth.

Target Reading Skill

Reread or Read Ahead Have you ever replayed a scene from a video or DVD so you could figure out what was going on? Rereading a passage is like doing this. Sometimes you may not understand a sentence or a paragraph the first time you read it. When this happens, go back and read it again. Sometimes you may need to reread it two or more times.

Reading ahead can help you understand something you are not sure of in the text. If you do not understand a word or passage, keep reading. The word or idea may be explained later.

For example, when you first see the word *degrees* under the heading "Five Ways to Look at Earth," you may not understand what it means. Most people think of how hot or cold something is when they read that word. If you read ahead, you will see that *degrees* is also a unit for measuring angles.

Vocabulary Strategy

Using Context Clues Words work together to explain meaning. The meaning of a word may depend on the words around it, or context. The context gives you clues to a word's meaning.

Try this example. Say that you do not understand the meaning of the word *movement* in the following passage:

The theme of <u>movement</u> tells you how people, goods, and ideas get from one place to another.

You could ask yourself: "What information does the passage give me about the word?" Answer: "I know that movement is how people, goods, and ideas get from one place to another. This tells me that movement must be a way of getting from place to place."

Section 1 Summary

The Study of Earth and Five Ways to Look at Earth

¹ Geography is the study of Earth. Five themes help geographers keep track of information about Earth and its people. These themes are: 1. location 2. regions 3. place 4. movement 5. human-environment interaction. They
⁵ help us see where things are, and why they are there. ✓

  1. Geographers study a place by finding its **location**. Geographers use cardinal directions to describe north, south, east, and west.

  Another way to describe location is to use latitude
¹⁰ and longitude. Latitude is the distance north or south of the Equator. Longitude is the distance east or west of the Prime Meridian. Latitude and longitude are measured in degrees.

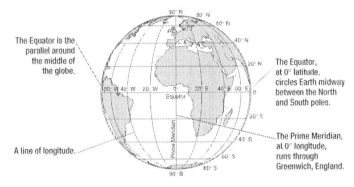

The Equator is the parallel around the middle of the globe.

A line of longitude.

The Equator, at 0° latitude, circles Earth midway between the North and South poles.

The Prime Meridian, at 0° longitude, runs through Greenwich, England.

  Lines of latitude, also called parallels, are east-west
¹⁵ circles around the globe. The latitude at 0 degrees (0°) is the Equator. Suppose you could cut Earth in half at the Equator. Each half of Earth is called a hemisphere. The Equator divides Earth into Northern and Southern hemispheres.

Key Terms

geography (jee AHG ru fee) *n.* the study of Earth
cardinal directions (KAHR duh nul duh REK shunz) *n.* the directions north, east, south, or west
latitude (LAT uh tood) *n.* the distance north or south of Earth's Equator, in degrees
longitude (LAHN juh tood) *n.* distance east or west of the Prime Meridian, in degrees
parallel (PA ruh lel) *n.* a line of latitude
hemisphere (HEM ih sfeer) *n.* half of Earth

What do the five themes of geography help us do?

_____

_____

_____

_____

Read ahead to see what kinds of things regions can have in common. Pick two to write down.

1. _____

2. _____

What kinds of things go from one place to another in the theme of movement?

_____

_____

_____

What does the word *environment* mean in the underlined sentence? Circle the words in this paragraph that could help you learn what *environment* means and write a definition below

_____

_____

20 Lines of longitude, also called meridians, run north and south. The Prime Meridian is the line of longitude that marks 0° of longitude. It divides Earth into Eastern and Western hemispheres.

Lines of longitude and latitude form a global grid.
25 Think of a tic-tac-toe game or a Bingo card. Geographers use this grid to state absolute location. The absolute location of a place is its exact address. For example, Savannah, Georgia, is located at 32° north latitude and 81° west longitude.

30 2. When places have something in common such as people, history, climate, or land, geographers call them **regions**. For example, the state you live in is a region because there is one government that unites the whole state.

35 3. Geographers also study **place**. Place includes both human and physical features at a specific location. You might say that the land is hilly. That is a physical feature. Or you might talk about how many people live in a place. That is a human feature.

40 4. The theme of **movement** tells you how people, goods, and ideas get from one place to another. For example, soccer is a popular game in parts of the United States. People who play soccer have moved here from other countries. This theme helps you under-
45 stand how and why things change. ✓

5. The last theme is **human-environment interac-tion.** It looks at how people change the world around them. It also looks at how the environment changes people.

Review Questions

1. What do geographers study?

_____

2. What is a hemisphere?

_____

_____

Key Terms

meridian (muh RID ee un) *n.* a line of longitude

CHAPTER 1

Prepare to Read

Section 2
The Geographer's Tools

Objectives

1. Find out how maps and globes show information about Earth's surface.
2. See how mapmakers show Earth's round surface on flat maps.
3. Learn how to read maps.

Target Reading Skill

Paraphrase When you paraphrase, you put something into your own words. If you can put something into your own words, it means that you understand what you have read. Paraphrasing will also help you remember what you have read.

For example, look at the first paragraph under the heading "Globes and Maps." You could paraphrase it this way:

A globe is the best way to show Earth. The main difference is the size.

As you read, paraphrase the information following each heading.

Vocabulary Strategy

Using Context to Clarify Meaning When you come across a word that you do not know, you may not need to look it up in a dictionary. In this workbook, key terms appear in blue. The definitions of the terms are in a box at the bottom of the page. If you stop to look at the definition, you interrupt your reading. Instead, continue to read to the end of the paragraph. See if you can figure out what the word means from the words around it. Then look at the definition at the bottom of the page to see how close you were. Finally, reread the paragraph to make sure you understood what you read.

Section 2 Summary

Globes and Maps

1 The best way to show Earth is to use a globe. A globe is a model of Earth with the same round shape. Using globes, mapmakers can show Earth's continents and oceans much as they really are. The only difference is 5 the scale.

There is a problem with globes, though. A globe big enough to show the streets of your town would be huge. It would be too big to put in your pocket.

Because of that problem, people use flat maps. But maps have problems, too. Earth is round. A map is flat. It is impossible to show Earth on a flat surface without distortion. Something will look too large or too small. Or it will be in the wrong place. Mapmakers have found ways to limit these distortions. ✓

15 Where do mapmakers get the information they need to make a map? To make a map, mapmakers measure the ground. They also use photographs taken from planes and satellite images. Satellite images are pictures of Earth's surface taken from a satellite. Both 20 provide current information about Earth's surface.

Geographers also use computer software. A Geographic information system, or GIS, is useful to governments and businesses as well.

Getting It All on the Map

In 1569, a mapmaker named Gerardus Mercator (juh 25 RAHR dus mur KAY tur) made a map for sailors. Mercator wanted to make a map that would help sailors find land. His map showed directions accurately. But sizes and distances were distorted. The Mercator projection is still used today.

Target Reading Skill

Paraphrase the bracketed paragraph in less than 25 words.

_____

_____

_____

✓ Reading Check

What are the advantages and disadvantages of two ways of showing Earth's surface?

Globes

Advantage: _____

_____

Disadvantage: _____

_____

Maps

Advantage: _____

_____

Disadvantage: _____

_____

Key Terms

scale (SKAYL) *n.* relative size
distortion (dih STAWR shun) *n.* loss of accuracy
Geographic information systems (jee uh GRAF ik in fur MAY shun SIS tumz) *n.* computer-based systems that provide information about locations
projection (proh JEK shun) *n.* a way to map Earth on a flat surface

³⁰ On a globe, the lines of longitude meet at the poles. To make a flat map, Mercator had to stretch the spaces between the lines of longitude. On the map, land near the Equator was about the right size. But land areas near the poles became much larger. <u>Geographers call</u> ³⁵ <u>the Mercator projection a conformal map.</u> It shows correct shapes, but not true distances or sizes.

Another kind of map is named for its designer, Arthur Robinson. The Robinson projection shows most distances, sizes, and shapes accurately. Even so, there ⁴⁰ are distortions, especially around the edges of the map. It is one of the most popular maps today. ✓

Reading Maps

All maps have the same basic parts. They have a compass rose that shows ⁴⁵ direction. They have a scale bar. It shows how distances on the map compare to actual distances on the land. And they have a key, or legend. It explains the ⁵⁰ map's symbols and shading. ✓

Key

——— State border

🛡 Interstate highway

🛡 U.S. route

★ State capital

• Other city

0 miles   100

0 kilometers   100

Lambert Azimuthal Equal Area

Review Questions

1. Where do mapmakers get the information they need to make a map?

_____

_____

2. Which map projection would a sailor most likely use?

_____

_____

Key Terms

compass rose (KUM pus rohz) *n.* a diagram of a compass showing direction

key (kee) *n.* the part of a map that explains the symbols

Find the underlined sentence. From context clues, write a definition of *conformal map*. Circle words or phrases in the text that helped you write your definition.

_____

_____

_____

✓ Reading Check

Where is the distortion on a Robinson map?

_____

_____

_____

✓ Reading Check

What do the different parts of a map tell you?

Compass rose: _____

_____

Scale bar: _____

_____

Key: _____

_____

1. Which of the following is NOT a tool a geographer would use to study location?
   A. cardinal directions
   B. climate
   C. lines of latitude
   D. degrees

2. The theme geographers use to group places that have something in common is
   A. location.
   B. regions.
   C. place.
   D. movement.

3. What disadvantages do all flat maps share?
   A. They have some sort of distortion.
   B. They are hard to carry.
   C. There are few sources to create them.
   D. They can only show areas at a small scale.

4. Which of the following do mapmakers use to make maps?
   A. ground surveys
   B. aerial photographs and satellite images
   C. Geographic information systems
   D. all of the above

5. What basic parts do all maps share?
   A. compass rose
   B. scale
   C. key
   D. all of the above

Short Answer Question

Which would be more helpful for studying the exact shapes of continents, a globe or a map? Why?

_____

_____

_____

_____

Prepare to Read

Section 1 Our Planet, Earth

Objectives

1. Learn about Earth's movement around the sun.
2. Explore seasons and latitude.

Target Reading Skill

Use Context Clues What should you do when you come across a word you don't know? Or, what if the word looks familiar, but its meaning is unclear to you? Then, look for clues to help you. Context clues are the words, phrases, and sentences around the unfamiliar word.

The word *revolution* is on the next page. Maybe the last time you saw that word it meant a rebellion. In this section, it means something very different. Use the context clues to help you figure out the meaning of revolution.

Vocabulary Strategy

Recognize Signal Words Signal words are words or phrases that prepare you for what is coming next. They are like road signs that tell drivers what to look for on the road ahead. In this section you will learn how Earth travels around the sun. You will also learn how the movement of Earth causes day, night, and the different seasons. Look out for signal words and phrases such as *then, next, as a result, for this reason,* and *as.* They will help you understand how one thing, such as the movement of Earth, leads to another thing, such as why it is morning in New York hours before it is morning in Utah.

Earth and the Sun

1 The sun is about 93 million miles (150 million kilometers) away. But it still provides Earth with heat and light. If you were to trace the path that Earth makes as it moves around the sun, your finger would trace a circle. Instead of saying Earth circles the sun, we say that Earth orbits the sun. It takes one year to complete one revolution around the sun.

As Earth orbits the sun, it also turns on its axis. Each rotation takes about 24 hours. As Earth rotates, it is night on the side away from the sun. As that side turns toward the sun, the sun appears to rise. It is daytime on the side of Earth that faces the sun. As that side turns away from the sun, the sun appears to set. ✓

Earth rotates toward the east, so the day starts earlier in the east. Governments have divided the world into standard time zones. Time zones are usually one hour apart.

Seasons and Latitude

Imagine sticking a pencil through an orange. The pencil is the axis, the orange is Earth. If you tilt or lean the pencil, then the orange tilts too. <u>Earth is tilted on its axis.</u> At different times in Earth's orbit, the Northern Hemisphere may be tilted toward or away from the sun. At other times, neither hemisphere is tilted toward or away from the sun. Earth has seasons because it is tilted during the revolutions.

Let's call the eraser end of the pencil the Northern Hemisphere and the sharpened end the Southern Hemisphere. For several months of the year as Earth orbits the sun, the Northern Hemisphere (eraser end) is tilted toward the sun. The Northern Hemisphere

---

✓ Reading Check

Explain why it is day on one side of Earth and night on the other side.

_____

_____

_____

⟳ Target Reading Skill

Read the underlined sentence. Circle words in the context that tell you what _tilted_ means. Write a definition on the lines below.

tilted: _____

_____

_____

Key Terms

orbit (AWR bit) _n._ path one body makes as it circles around another
revolution (rev uh LOO shun) _n._ circular motion
axis (AK sis) _n._ an imaginary line through Earth between the North and South poles, around which Earth turns
rotation (roh TAY shun) _n._ a complete turn

receives lots of direct sunlight. That creates spring and summer in the Northern Hemisphere. At the same time, the Southern Hemisphere (the sharpened end) is tilted away from the sun. The Southern Hemisphere
35 receives indirect sunlight, creating fall and winter in the Southern Hemisphere.

When the Northern Hemisphere is tilted toward the sun, the Southern Hemisphere is tilted away. For this reason, the seasons are reversed in the Southern Hemisphere.

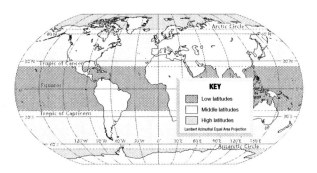

How far a place is from the Equator influences the temperature of a place. Remember that lines of latitude circle Earth above and below the Equator. The areas between the Tropic of Cancer and the Tropic of
45 Capricorn receive fairly direct sunlight all year. Weather is usually hot.

The areas above the Arctic Circle and below the Antarctic Circle get indirect sun. They are cool or very cold all year.
50 The areas between the high and low latitudes are the middle latitudes. In summer, they get fairly direct sunlight. In winter, they get indirect sunlight. This means they have four seasons. Summers are hot, winters are cold, and spring and fall are in between. ✔

Review Questions

1. What is the rotation of Earth?

_____

_____

2. How do Earth's tilt and orbit cause the seasons?

_____

_____

_____

In the bracketed paragraph, a signal phrase is used to show effect. Find the signal phrase and circle it. What effect is explained?

_____

_____

_____

✓ Reading Check

How does latitude influence temperature?

_____

_____

_____

Objectives

1. Learn about the planet Earth.
2. Explore the forces inside Earth.
3. Explore the forces on Earth's surface.

Target Reading Skill

Use Context Clues When you come across a word you don't know, you can often use context to figure out its meaning. Context clues can be a definition, an example, an explanation, or even what you already know about the subject.

The phrase *Ring of Fire* appears in this section. Which box in the graphic organizer will help you the most as you try to figure out the meaning of *Ring of Fire?*

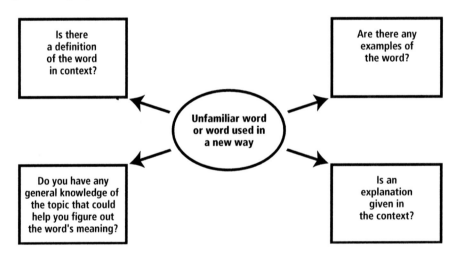

Is there a definition of the word in context?

Are there any examples of the word?

Unfamiliar word or word used in a new way

Do you have any general knowledge of the topic that could help you figure out the word's meaning?

Is an explanation given in the context?

Vocabulary Strategy

Recognize Signal Words When someone drives on a road or highway, road signs can help them know whether to drive fast or slowly, when traffic will merge, and what to watch out for on the road ahead. Recognizing signal words is a lot like reading road signs. Signal words tell you what to expect.

Some signal words show different kinds of relationships, such as contrast. Contrast shows the difference between things or ideas.

Signal words that show contrast include *but, however, not, on the other hand, even though, yet,* and *despite.*

Section 2 Summary

Understanding Earth

1 Deep inside Earth is a core of hot metal. Around that is a second layer called the mantle. A third layer floating on top of the mantle is called the crust. The surface, or top of the crust, includes Earth's land areas and ocean 5 floors. Powerful forces shape and change Earth. ✓

Most of Earth's surface is not land however. It is water. In fact, water covers more than 70 percent of Earth. The oceans hold about 97 percent of Earth's water. That means that most of Earth's water is salty. 10 Most of the fresh water is frozen. People can use only a small part of Earth's fresh water. It comes from lakes, rivers, and ground water. They receive water from rain.

Above Earth's surface is the atmosphere, a thick layer of gases. The atmosphere contains oxygen that 15 people and animals need to breathe. It also has the gas that plants need.

Earth's land surface comes in all shapes and sizes. Mountains, volcanoes, hills, plateaus, and plains are landforms found on the top of the crust. Mountains 20 rise more than 2,000 feet (610 meters) above sea level. A volcano is a kind of mountain. Hills are lower and less steep than mountains. A plateau is a large, mostly flat area that rises above the land around it. Plains are large areas of flat or gently rolling land.

Forces Inside Earth

25 Extreme heat deep inside Earth is always changing the way Earth looks on the surface. It makes rocks rise toward the surface. Streams of hot magma push up Earth's crust to form volcanoes. Volcanoes pour out molten rock, or lava, from inside Earth.

30 Streams of hot magma may also push the crust apart along openings called seams. These seams separate

✓ Reading Check

Which layer of Earth contains all of its landforms?

_____

_____

_____

⊙ Target Reading Skill

If you do not know what the word *atmosphere* means, notice that a definition follows the phrase in the underlined sentence. What does *atmosphere* mean?

_____

_____

_____

Key Terms

core (kawr) *n.* the sphere of very hot metal at the center of Earth

mantle (MAN tul) *n.* the thick layer around Earth's core

crust (krust) *n.* the thin, rocky layer on Earth's surface

magma (MAG muh) *n.* soft, nearly molten rock

huge blocks of crust called plates. A plate may include continents or parts of continents. A plate also includes part of the ocean floor.

35   Sometimes, where two plates meet, molten rock explodes to the surface through a volcano. A good example of this is the Ring of Fire. It is a string of volcanoes near the plates that form the Pacific Ocean. Volcanoes can form at other places, too.

40   When two plates push together, the crust cracks and splinters. These cracks are called faults. When blocks of crust rub against each other along faults, they release energy in the form of earthquakes.

    Scientists now know that the forces inside Earth are 45 powerful enough to move continents. They know that the continents were once close together. Magma works to move Earth's plates and continents. ✓

Forces on Earth's Surface

Forces inside Earth slowly build up Earth's crust. But two forces slowly wear down the surface. Weathering is one force. Water, ice, and living things like lichens on rocks slowly break rocks into tiny pieces. Weathering helps create soil. Soil is made up of tiny pieces of rock mixed with decaying animal and plant matter.

    Erosion also reshapes Earth's surface and land-55 forms. Water and wind carry soil downstream or downwind to create new landforms. Plains are often made of soil carried by rivers. ✓

Review Questions

1. What are Earth's three main layers?

_____

_____

2. How is erosion different from weathering?

_____

_____

✓ Reading Check

How do continents move apart?

_____

_____

_____

Vocabulary Strategy

In the bracketed paragraph, a signal word is used to show contrast. Find the signal word and circle it. What is being contrasted here?

_____

_____

_____

✓ Reading Check

What is a landform made from weathering and erosion?

_____

_____

_____

Key Terms

plate (playt) *n.* a huge block of Earth's crust

weathering (WETH ur ing) *n.* a process that breaks rocks down into small pieces

erosion (ee ROH zhun) *n.* the removal of small pieces of rock by water, ice, or wind

Objectives

1. Learn about weather and climate.
2. Explore latitude, landforms, and precipitation.
3. Discover how oceans affect climate.

Target Reading Skill

Use Context Clues When you read, you sometimes come across a word you don't know. Sometimes the word you don't know is used in comparison with a word or a group of words you *do* know. These word clues and your own general knowledge can help you figure out what the word means without having to look it up.

Look at this sentence:

The kindling burned more quickly than the other pieces of wood.

Here, the word *kindling* is compared to <u>other pieces of wood.</u> Reading the sentence will help you figure out the meaning of the new word.

Vocabulary Strategy

Recognize Signal Words Signal words are words or phrases that give you clues or directions when reading. Sometimes a signal word or phrase will alert you that two or more things are being compared. Here are some words that can signal a comparison.

also	like	same as
as well as	more	similar to
both	same	too
in the same way	just as	less

Weather or Climate?

[1] Do you check the weather before you get ready for school? Most people need to know the weather before they get dressed. They need to know two things. The first is temperature, the second is precipitation. The [5] temperature is how hot or cold the air is. Precipitation is water that falls to the ground as rain, sleet, hail, or snow. Weather is not the same as climate. Weather is what people feel from day to day. Climate is the average weather from year to year. ✓

Why Climates Vary

[10] Earth has many climates. Some climates are so hot that people almost always wear summer clothes. In some climates, snow stays on the ground most of the year. Climate depends on location. Places in low latitudes, or the tropics, have hot climates. This is because they are [15] closer to the Equator and get direct sunlight. Places in the high latitudes, or polar regions, have cold climates. That is because their sunlight is indirect. ✓

Air and water spread heat around Earth as they move. Without wind and water, places in the tropics [20] would overheat. Oceans take longer than land to heat up and cool down. This makes land near oceans have mild temperatures.

Oceans and Climates

An ocean current is like a huge river in the ocean. Ocean currents move across great distances. The cur- [25] rents are huge rivers of warm and cold water. Usually, warm water flows away from the Equator. Cold water moves toward the Equator.

✓ Reading Check

How is climate different from weather?

_____

_____

_____

✓ Reading Check

Which has a colder climate, high latitudes or low latitudes? Why?

_____

_____

_____

🎯 Target Reading Skill

If you do not know what ocean currents are, notice that they are compared to huge rivers in the ocean. How does the comparison help you find the meaning?

_____

_____

_____

Key Terms

weather (WETH ur) *n.* the condition of the air and sky from day to day

temperature (TEM pur uh chur) *n.* how hot or cold the air is

precipitation (pree sip uh TAY shun) *n.* water that falls to the ground as rain, sleet, hail, or snow

climate (KLY mut) *n.* the average weather over many years

Ocean currents help make climates milder. A warm current can make a cool place warmer. A cold current can make a warm place cooler. The warm Gulf Stream gives Western Europe a milder climate than it would if the current was not near. In the same way, the cold Peru Current keeps Antofagasta, Chile, cooler than it would otherwise be.

35 Oceans and lakes affect climate in other ways, too. Water takes longer to heat or cool than land. In summer, wind blowing over water cools the nearby land. In the winter, water helps keep nearby land by the shore warmer than inland areas. ✓

Raging Storms

40 Wind and water can make climates milder. They can also create dangerous storms. Tropical cyclones are a good example. Similar storms that form over the Atlantic Ocean are usually called hurricanes. Their winds can reach speeds of more than 100 miles (160 45 kilometers) per hour. Hurricanes push huge amounts of water onto land, destroying homes and towns.

Tornadoes are like funnels of wind. They can reach 200 miles (320 kilometers) per hour. The swirling winds wreck almost everything in their path. They are 50 just as dangerous as hurricanes. But they affect much smaller areas. ✓

Other storms are less dangerous. In winter, blizzards dump snow on parts of North America. Heavy rainstorms and thunderstorms happen in the spring 55 and summer.

Review Questions

1. What kind of climate occurs near the Equator?

_____

_____

2. How does the ocean influence the temperature of land near it?

_____

_____

> **Key Terms**
> **tropical cyclone** (TRAHP ih kul SY klohn) *n.* an intense wind and rain storm that forms over oceans in the tropics

In the bracketed paragraph, a signal phrase is used to make a comparison. Find the phrase and circle it. What is being compared here?

_____

_____

✓ **Reading Check**

During the summer, are places near the ocean hotter or cooler than places inland?

_____

_____

✓ **Reading Check**

Which storms cover larger areas, hurricanes or tornadoes?

_____

_____

Prepare to Read

Section 4
How Climate Affects Vegetation

Objectives

1. Investigate climate and vegetation.
2. Explore Earth's vegetation regions.
3. Study vertical climate zones.

Target Reading Skill

Use Context Clues What can you do when you see a word used in an unfamiliar way? Of course, you could look the word up in a dictionary. But often you can get a good idea of what the word means from the words around it.

Textbooks often give examples of new words or ideas. You can tell the meaning of the word from the examples. In the sentence below, the meaning of the word *scrub* is given by the examples in italics:

Scrub includes *bushes and small trees.*

Did you figure out that *scrub* is a word that describes types of plants?

Vocabulary Strategy

Recognize Signal Words Signal words are words or phrases that give you clues or directions when reading. They tell you that what is coming next will be different in some way from what you have just read.

Sometimes a signal word or phrase will help you recognize a cause or effect.

Words that signal causes:	Words that signal effects:
because	as a result
if	so
since	then
on account of	therefore

Climate and Vegetation

1 These are the five major types of climate: tropical, dry, temperate marine, temperate continental, and polar. Every climate has its own types of natural vegetation. That is because different plants need different amounts
5 of water and sunlight and different temperatures to live. ✓

You can probably guess that a **tropical climate** is hot! Some tropical climates also get rain all year long. You would find a tropical rain forest in this climate.
10 Other tropical climates get less rain. In those climates there is more grass and fewer trees.

Dry climates have very hot summers and mild winters. Because dry climates get little rain, few plants can grow there. Semidry climates get just enough rain to grow scrub, including bushes and small trees.

Temperate marine climates are usually near a coastline. There are three types: Mediterranean, marine west coast, and humid subtropical. All have mild winters. The marine west coast and humid subtropical climates
20 get lots of rain. The Mediterranean climates get less rain and have Mediterranean vegetation.

The summers in **temperate continental climates** can be hot. But the winters are very cold. Grasslands and forests grow in these climates.
25 **Polar climates** are always cold. Summers are short and cool there. Winters are long and very cold. In the polar climates you find the tundra and ice caps.

Earth's Vegetation Regions

Vegetation depends on climate. But other things, such as soil, also affect vegetation. Geographers have
30 grouped vegetation into several regions. We will study just a few of them here.

✓ Reading Check

Why does each climate have its own type of vegetation?

_____

_____

_____

Vocabulary Strategy

In the bracketed paragraph, a signal word is used to show cause and effect. Find the signal word and circle it. Then write the cause and effect below.

Cause: _____

Effect: _____

Key Terms

vegetation (vej uh TAY shun) *n.* plants that grow in a region
tundra (TUN druh) *n.* an area of cold climate and low-lying vegetation

_____

_____

_____

Target Reading Skill

Underline the words in the bracketed paragraph that help you to figure out the meaning of the term *coniferous forest*. Then complete the following sentence:

Trees in coniferous forests have

_____.

What is the meaning of the word coniferous? What context clues helped you figure out the meaning? Write the context clues on the line below.

_____

_____

✓ Reading Check

How does vegetation change with elevation?

_____

_____

Tropical Rain Forest Plentiful sunlight, heat, and rain cause thousands of plants to grow. The trees grow so tall and close together they form a canopy high in
35 the air. Smaller plants grow in the shade.

Tropical Savanna Some tropical areas have less rain. They have a landscape of grasslands and scattered trees known as savanna.

Desert Scrub Some very dry areas have just enough
40 rain to support plant growth called desert scrub. ✓

Deciduous forest Several different climates support forests of deciduous trees. Many people enjoy the changing colors of leaves in the fall.

Coniferous forest Trees with needles instead of leaves can grow in climates that are a little drier than those needed by leafy trees. Coniferous trees get their name from the cones they produce.

Vertical Climate Zones

Mountains have vertical climate zones. That means that climate and vegetation depend on how high the
50 mountain is. In a tropical region, plants that need a tropical climate will grow only near the bottom of a mountain. Farther up you will find plants that can grow in a temperate climate. Near the top you will only find plants that grow in a polar climate. ✓

Review Questions

1. What are the five main types of climate?

_____

_____

2. What landform has a vertical climate zone?

_____

_____

Key Terms

canopy (KAN uh pea) *n.* the layer formed by the uppermost branches of a rain forest
savanna (suh VAN uh) *n.* a parklike combination of grasslands and scattered trees
desert scrub (DEZ urt skrub) *n.* desert plants that need little water
deciduous trees (dee SIJ oo us treez) *n.* trees that lose their leaves seasonally
coniferous trees (koh NIF ur us treez) *n.* trees that produce cones to carry seeds

1. When it is summer in the Northern Hemisphere, it is
   _____ in the Southern Hemisphere.
   A. summer
   B. winter
   C. spring
   D. fall

2. The layers of Earth include
   A. core, water, crust.
   B. volcanoes, mountains, plateaus.
   C. lava, magma, plates.
   D. core, mantle, crust.

3. Weathering is caused by
   A. water.
   B. ice.
   C. lichens.
   D. all of the above

4. Which of the following influences climate?
   A. latitude
   B. longitude
   C. the Prime Meridian
   D. tornadoes

5. In which vegetation region would you find trees that lose their leaves
   seasonally?
   A. tropical rain forest
   B. coniferous forest
   C. deciduous forest
   D. tundra

Short Answer Question

Why do some coastal cities in the tropics stay cool?

_____

_____

_____

_____

_____

CHAPTER 3

Prepare to Read

Section 1 Population

Objectives

1. Learn about population distribution.
2. Explore population density.
3. Investigate population growth.

Target Reading Skill

Comparison and Contrast Have you ever played the game where you try to find the differences between two pictures? The pictures seem to be the same, but if you look closely, you can find little differences. Sometimes the differences are easy to spot. Other times you really have to work at it.

Playing that game is similar to comparing and contrasting as you read. It is easy to see the difference between the terms *birthrate* and *death rate.* But terms like *population density* and *population distribution* will require a little more work.

Vocabulary Strategy

Recognize Roots When you add letters in front or to the end of a root word, you create a new word. You use roots all the time without even thinking about it. When you write, "I watched a movie last night," you knew to add *-ed* to *watch* to create *watched*.

The word *density* appears in this section. The root word is *dense*. The letters *-ity* have been added. But the word isn't spelled *denseity*! It is spelled *density*. Sometimes the root word changes when you add letters. See if you can find more examples as you read. *Hint:* There is one in the first sentence of the next page.

Section 1 Summary

Population Distribution

The way Earth's population is spread out is called population distribution. People tend to live in uneven clusters on Earth's surface. Demography tries to explain why populations change and why population distribution is uneven.

People usually don't move without a good reason. As long as people can make a living where they are, they usually stay there. That means that regions with large populations tend to keep them.

In the past, most people lived on farms where they grew their own food. Therefore, more people lived in places that had good climates for growing crops. After about 1800, things changed. Railroads and steamships made traveling long distances much easier. People moved to cities to work in factories and offices instead of working on farms. ✓

Population Density

How do you find out how crowded a place really is? Find out how many people live in an area. Then divide that number by the area's square miles or square kilometers. That will give you the population density. Remember, population distribution tells you the actual number of people in an area. Population density tells you the average number of people in an area.

Some places are more crowded, or have a higher population density than others. For example, Japan has a high population density, while Canada has a low population density. ✓

Key Terms

population (pahp yuh LAY shun) *n.* total number of people in an area

population distribution (pahp yoo LAY shun dis truh byoo shun) *n.* the way the population is spread out over an area

demography (dih MAH gruh fee) *n.* the science that studies population distribution and change

population density (pahp yuh LAY shun DEN suh tee) *n.* the average number of people per square mile or square kilometer

---

Vocabulary Strategy

Each of the underlined words to the left contains another word that is its root. Circle the roots you find in these words. The root of the first word, *uneven*, is *even*.

✓ Reading Check

What happened to make people move to the cities after 1800?

_____

_____

_____

Target Reading Skill

How is population density different from population distribution?

_____

_____

_____

_____

✓ Reading Check

Which country is more crowded, Japan or Canada? How do you know?

_____

_____

_____

_____

Population Growth

For thousands of years, the world's population grew slowly. Food supplies were scarce. People lived with-
30 out clean water and waste removal. Millions died of diseases. Although the birthrate was high, so was the death rate. The life expectancy, or the average length of people's lives, was short.

Today, death rates have dropped sharply. In some
35 countries, birthrates have increased. As a result, populations have grown very fast. At the same time, people live longer than ever. Scientific progress caused much of this change. See the chart below to learn more. ✓

✓ Reading Check

Why have populations risen rapidly in recent years?

_____

_____

_____

Scientific Progress	
Changes in health and medicine	Green Revolution—improvements in farming methods
Clean drinking water / Vaccines and medicine	Ways to grow more food / Ways to grow food with less water

People in many countries still face big problems.
40 Some nations do not have enough fresh water. In parts of Asia and Africa, the population is growing faster than the food supply.

The way people live can be hurt by population growth. There are shortages of jobs, schools, and hous-
45 ing. Public services like transportation and sanitation are inadequate. Forests are disappearing. This causes still more problems.

Review Questions

1. How did the Green Revolution increase population?

_____

_____

2. List problems caused by population growth.

_____

_____

Key Terms

birthrate (BURTH rayt) *n.* the number of live births each year per 1,000 people

death rate (deth rayt) *n.* the number of deaths each year per 1,000 people

Objectives

1. Learn about migration, or people's movement from one region to another.
2. Investigate urbanization, or people's movement to cities.

Target Reading Skill

Identify Contrasts Contrast is the way that things are different from each other. Some contrasts are easy to see. For example, it is easy to see how the city is different from the country. The city has more buildings, more people. The country has more plants and trees.

Ideas can be contrasted too. Sometimes it is harder to see the difference in ideas. On the next page you will read about the push-pull theory. Think about how the word *push* means something very different than the word *pull*. This will help you understand the push-pull theory.

Vocabulary Strategy

Find Roots Often, letters are added to the beginning or end of a word. The word the letters are added to is the root word. Sometimes the added letters will completely change the meaning of the root word.

For example, in this section you will study voluntary migration. This is a phrase that means "people choose to migrate." But add the letters *in-* to *voluntary* and you get something very different. *Involuntary migration* is a term that describes people who are forced to move.

Why People Migrate

¹For thousands of years, people have moved to new places. This movement is called migration. Immigrants are people who move into one country from another.

Some people choose to move. This is called volun-⁵tary migration. Today, most people move by their own choice. The push-pull theory explains voluntary migration. It says that difficulties "push" people to leave. At the same time, the hope for a better life "pulls" them to a new country. ☑

¹⁰Here is an example of the push-pull theory. Many years ago, 1.5 million people left Ireland for the United States. Disease had destroyed Ireland's main crop, potatoes. Hunger pushed people to migrate. Job opportunities pulled Irish families to the United States.

¹⁵Today, the main sources of migration are countries where many people are poor or there are few jobs. Sometimes, wars have made life dangerous and difficult. Also, some governments limit people's freedom. These problems push people to leave. They are pulled ²⁰by the possibility of good jobs or political freedom.

Sometimes people are forced to move. This is known as involuntary migration. In the 1800s, the British sent prisoners to Australia to serve their sentences. War also forces people to migrate to escape ²⁵death or danger.

The biggest involuntary migration may have been the slave trade. From the 1500s to the 1800s, millions of Africans were enslaved and taken to European colonies in North and South America.

✓ Reading Check

Why do people migrate?

_____

_____

_____

Target Reading Skill

How is involuntary migration different from voluntary migration?

_____

_____

_____

> **Key Terms**
> **migration** (my GRAY shun) *n.* the movement of people from one place or region to another
> **immigrants** (IM uh grunts) *n.* people who move into one country from another

Urbanization

30 Millions of people in many countries have moved to cities from farms and small villages. As a result, some cities have grown <u>enormously</u> in recent years. The movement of people to cities and the growth of cities is called <u>urbanization</u>.

35 In Europe and North America, the growth of industry created jobs. People moved to cities for jobs in factories and offices. Today, people in Europe and North America are moving out of cities into suburbs. Most people in suburbs rely on cars for <u>transportation</u>. More 40 cars mean increased pollution. But people still move to suburbs so they can own homes.

In Asia, Africa, and Latin America, people are still moving from the countryside to <u>growing</u> cities. Indonesia is an example. In the past, people lived in 45 rural areas. Recently, many Indonesians have moved to urban areas. The capital has grown from 3.9 million people to 11 million people in thirty years. ✓

Often, too many people are moving to the city too fast. Cities cannot provide the things that people 50 need. There are <u>shortages</u> of housing, jobs, schools, and hospitals.

So why do people move to big cities? As hard as life is in the cities, it can be even harder in the countryside. Often, there are few jobs and not enough farmland. 55 Most migrants who move to the city want a better life for their families.

Review Questions

1. Name one push factor and one pull factor.

_____

_____

2. What is urbanization?

_____

_____

Vocabulary Strategy

Each of the underlined words in the part titled "Urbanization" contains another word that is its root. Circle the roots in these words. The root of the first word, *enormously*, is *enormous*.

✓ Reading Check

How is the population of urban areas changing in Africa, Asia, and Latin America?

_____

_____

_____

_____

Objectives

1. Examine different kinds of economies.
2. Investigate levels of economic development.
3. Study global trade patterns.

Target Reading Skill

Make Comparisons Comparing two or more situations lets you see how they are alike. It is often easier to understand new facts by comparing them with facts you already know. Sometimes one thing is compared to several other things.

   In this section, you will read about developed nations and developing nations. As you read, compare how people live in developed and developing nations. What kinds of jobs do they have? What kinds of houses do they live in? Do people or machines do most of the work?

Vocabulary Strategy

Recognize Compound Words Compound words are made from two or more words. Compound words are like shortcuts. They make it easier to read or talk about things. For example, *workplace* is a compound word. You could say, "Describe the place where you work." Or, you could say, "Describe your workplace." If you know the meaning of the words that make up a compound word, you can often figure out the meaning of the compound word itself. Here are some compound words you will find in your reading.

sometimes	countryside
worldwide	anybody
healthcare	farmland

Section 3 Summary

Different Kinds of Economies

Economies differ from one country to another. However, in every economy, there are producers, who are the owners and workers who make products, and consumers who buy and use products.

The owner of the workplace usually decides how and what things will be made. But who are the owners? In some countries, the workplace belongs to private citizens. This economic system is called capitalism. In others, the government owns most workplaces. This is called communism.

Capitalism is also called a free-market economy. Producers compete freely for consumers' business. People may save money in banks, and invest money in a business.

Under communism, the government controls the prices of goods and services, what things are made, and how much workers are paid. Today, only a few nations practice communism. ✔

In some countries, the government owns some industries while others belong to private owners. This system is sometimes called a mixed economy.

Levels of Economic Development

Three hundred years ago, most people did work by hand. Then people invented machines to make goods. They used energy instead of people and animals to run machines. This was a new form of technology. Technology is a way of putting knowledge to practical use. This change in the way people made goods was called the Industrial Revolution.

Target Reading Skill

Compare producers and consumers. How are they different?

_____

_____

_____

✓ Reading Check

What are two differences between capitalism and communism?

1. _____

_____

2. _____

_____

Key Terms

economy (ih KAHN uh mee) *n.* a system in which people make, exchange, and use things that have value

producers (pruh DOOS urz) *n.* owners and workers

consumers (kun SOOM urz) *n.* people who buy and use products

capitalism (KAP ut ul iz um) *n.* an economic system in which individuals own most businesses

communism (KAHM yoo niz um) *n.* an economic system in which the central government owns most businesses

✓ **Reading Check**

How do developed nations differ from developing nations?

_____

_____

_____

Vocabulary Strategy

The word *healthcare* is a compound word. What are the two root words of *healthcare* and what does each root word mean?

1. _____

_____

2. _____

_____

Use the meanings above to understand the meaning of healthcare. Write a definition for healthcare on the lines below.

Healthcare means:

_____

_____

✓ **Reading Check**

What do developing nations sell to developed nations?

_____

_____

_____

The Industrial Revolution divided the world into developed nations and developing nations. People live differently in the two types of nations. Developed nations have more industries and a high level of technology. Developing nations have fewer industries and simpler technology. ✓

Only about one fifth of the world's people live in developed nations. These nations include the United States, Canada, Japan, and most of Europe. In these countries most people live in towns and cities. They work in offices and factories. Most people have enough food and water. Most people can get an education and healthcare. Developed nations have some problems. Two of these problems are unemployment and pollution.

Most of the people in the world live in developing nations. These nations are mainly in Africa, Asia, and Latin America. Most people grow just enough food for themselves. People and animals do most of the work. There are many problems in these nations. They include disease, food shortages, and political unrest.

World Trade Patterns

Different countries have different economic strengths. Countries trade with one another to get the things they want and need.

Countries have grown to depend on one another. Developing nations tend to sell foods, natural resources, and simple industrial products. In return, they buy high-technology goods from developed countries. ✓

Review Questions

1. How did the Industrial Revolution change the way people made things?

_____

_____

2. How do countries depend on one another?

_____

_____

Key Terms

developed nations (dih VEL upt NAY shunz) *n.* nations with many industries and advanced technology

developing nations (dih VEL up ing NAY shunz) *n.* nations with few industries and simple technology

Objectives

1. Examine different types of states.
2. Investigate types of government.
3. Learn about alliances and international organizations.

Target Reading Skill

Use Contrast Signal Words Signal words are words or phrases that give you clues when reading.

There are different kinds of signal words. Certain words, such as *like* or *unlike, just as* or even the phrase *such as* in the beginning of this sentence can signal a comparison or contrast. This section contrasts several kinds of government. You will learn that some governments encourage people to participate, other governments do not.

In the sentence below, are the signal words signaling comparison or contrast?

Just as in an absolute monarchy, dictatorships do not allow people to participate in government.

Once you read the section you will know for sure!

Vocabulary Strategy

Find Roots Often, syllables or groups of syllables are added at the beginning or end of a word to make a new word.

In some cases, the spelling changes slightly when a word becomes a root. Often, a final *e* is dropped when a new ending is added to a word.

Here are some other examples from this section.

Root	Added letters	New word
make	-ing	making
share	-ing	sharing
simple	-y	simply

The second sentence in the bracketed paragraph begins with the word *Some*. The fourth sentence begins with *Others*. These words signal a contrast. What contrast is made here?

_____

_____

✓ Reading Check

Name four kinds of states.

1. _____

2. _____

3. _____

4. _____

Vocabulary Strategy

Each of the four words below appear in the sections titled "Types of Government," and "International Organizations." Each contains a root that has had a spelling change before the ending was added. Write the full roots on the lines below.

1. earliest _____

2. dictator _____

3. alliance _____

4. organization _____

Types of States

1 When people lived in small groups, all adults took part in making group decisions. Today, nations are too large for everyone to take part in every decision. But they still need to be able to protect people. They need to be able
5 to solve problems. That is why we have governments.

A state is a region that shares a government. The entire United States can also be called a state. That's because it is a region that shares a federal government.

There are four kinds of states. Some regions are dependencies. They belong to another state. Others, like the United States, are nation-states, which are often simply called nations. Every place in the world where people live is a nation-state or dependency.

The first states formed in Southwest Asia more than
15 5,000 years ago. Early cities set up governments called city-states. Later, military leaders conquered several countries and ruled them as empires. ✓

Types of Government

Each state has a government. There are many different kinds of government. Some are controlled by one per-
20 son. Others are controlled by all of the people.

The earliest governments were simple. People lived in small groups. They practiced **direct democracy**. All adults took part in decisions. In time, communities banded together into larger tribal groups. Members of
25 the tribe had a say in group decisions. But under **tribal rule,** chiefs or elders made the final decision.

Key Terms

government (GUV urn munt) *n.* a body that makes laws
state (stayt) *n.* a region that shares a government
dependency (dee PEN dun see) *n.* a region that belongs to another state
nation-state (NAY shun stayt) *n.* a state that is independent of other states
city-state (SIH tee stayt) *n.* a small city-centered state
empire (EM pyr) *n.* a state containing several countries

Until about 200 years ago, **absolute monarchy** was one of the most common forms of government. In that system, kings or queens have complete control. Today, there are other countries where just one person rules. The leader is not a king or queen but a **dictator**. Dictators have complete control over a country. An **oligarchy** is a government controlled by a small group of people. The group may be the leaders of a political party, a group of military officers, or even a group of religious leaders. In oligarchies and dictatorships, ordinary people have little say in decisions. ✓

Today, most monarchies are **constitutional monarchies**. The power of the king or queen is limited by law. These nations have constitutions that define the government's power. **Representative democracies** are governments in which people elect representatives who create laws. If they do not like what a representative does, they can refuse to reelect that person.

International Organizations

Nations may agree to work together in an <u>alliance</u>. Members of an alliance are called allies. In some alliances, members agree to protect each other in case of attack. Some alliances, such as the European Union, are mainly economic.

The United Nations is an international organization that tries to resolve problems and promote peace. Almost all of the world's nations belong to the United Nations. It sponsors other international organizations with specific purposes, such as combating hunger or promoting the well-being of children. ✓

Review Questions

1. What were the earliest types of states?

_____

_____

2. What is an alliance?

_____

_____

✓ **Reading Check**

Name two forms of government in which the leader has total control.

1. _____

   _____

2. _____

   _____

✓ **Reading Check**

What is the purpose of the United Nations?

_____

_____

_____

Key Terms

constitution (kahn stuh TOO shuhn) *n.* a set of laws that define and often limit a government's power

1. The number of people per square mile or square kilometer is a region's
   A. population.
   B. population density.
   C. population distribution.
   D. life expectancy.

2. People moving to a different region to seek better job opportunities is an example of
   A. urbanization.
   B. suburbanization.
   C. voluntary migration.
   D. involuntary migration.

3. In which of the following does the government control the prices of goods and services?
   A. developed countries
   B. developing countries
   C. capitalism
   D. communism

4. In the earliest societies, the form of government was
   A. direct democracy.
   B. representative democracy.
   C. absolute monarchy.
   D. constitutional monarch.

5. Today, most monarchies are
   A. absolute monarchies.
   B. dictatorships.
   C. oligarchies.
   D. constitutional monarchies.

Short Answer Question

What is the Green Revolution?

_____

_____

_____

_____

_____

CHAPTER 4

Prepare to Read

Section 1
Understanding Culture

Objectives

1. Learn about culture.
2. Explore how culture has developed.

Target Reading Skill

Understand Sequence History is a series of events. To help you understand history, list events in sequence, or the order in which they happened. Make a chart like the one below to help you. This one is about how culture developed. The first two events are filled in for you. Fill in the event that happens next when you come across it as you read. The arrows show how one event leads to another.

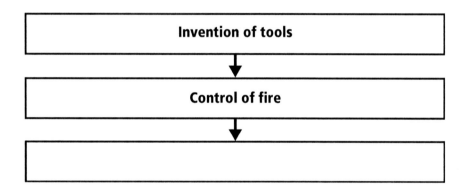

Vocabulary Strategy

Use Context Clues to Determine Meaning Context clues help you figure out the meaning of words. One way to use context clues is to imagine a blank space in place of the word you don't understand. Let's say you don't know the meaning of the word *institutions*. Read the paragraph below. There is a blank everywhere the word *institutions* would appear.

> Before civilizations developed, people had simple _____.
> These were extended families and councils of elders. As people gathered in larger groups, they needed more complex _____.
> They developed religions. States needed armies, schools, and governments. Today, we have many different kinds of _____. They are important parts of our culture.

Did you figure out that *institutions* means organized groups of people?

What Is Culture?

[1] Culture is the way people live. It includes what people believe and the things they do everyday. It includes the language people speak and the clothes they wear.

[5] Parents pass culture on to their children. Ideas and ways of doing things are called cultural traits. For example, in the United States, eating with a fork is a cultural trait. In Japan, people use chopsticks.

Some parts of a culture are easy to see. They include houses, food, and clothing. Things you cannot see or [10] touch are also part of culture. They include spiritual beliefs, government, and ideas about right and wrong. Language is a very important part of culture.

Geographers want to know how the environment affects culture. Japan is a nation of mountainous [15] islands, with very little farmland. So the Japanese use the sea for food. But the same environment may not lead to the same culture. Greece is also made of mountainous islands. The Greeks eat some fish. But they use mountainsides to get food. Goats and sheep graze [20] there and provide food for the Greeks. ✓

The cultural landscape varies from place to place. In Indonesia, farmers have used technology to carve terraces into hillsides. On the plains of northern India, farmers have laid out broad, flat fields.

The Development of Culture

[25] Scientists think that early cultures went through four important steps. First was the invention of tools. Second was the control of fire. Third was the beginnings of farming. Fourth was the development of civilizations.

✓ Reading Check

Describe the way environment affects culture.

_____

_____

_____

Vocabulary Strategy

The word *landscape* has more than one meaning. You may already know one of its meanings. Circle the words in the bracketed paragraph that are context clues for *landscape*. What does it mean in this context?

_____

_____

_____

Key Terms

culture (KUL chur) *n.* the way of life of a people, including their beliefs and practices

cultural landscape (KUL chur ul LAND skayp) *n.* the parts of a people's environment that they have shaped and the technology they have used to shape it

civilization (sih vuh luh ZAY shun) *n.* an advanced culture with cities and a system of writing

---

Early people were hunters and gatherers. They trav-
30 eled from place to place. As they traveled, they collect-
ed wild plants, hunted animals, and fished. Later, they
learned to grow crops. They tamed wild animals to
help them work or to use for food. Over time, people
got more of their food from farming. This is called the
35 Agricultural Revolution.

Farmers were able to grow more food than they
needed. This meant that some people could work full
time on crafts such as metalworking. They traded the
things they made for food. People developed laws and
40 government. To keep track of things, they developed
writing. All these events together created the first civilizations. That was about 5,000 years ago. ✅

In time, farming and civilization spread throughout
the world. Then, about 200 years ago, people invented
45 power-driven machinery. This was the beginning of the
Industrial Revolution. It led to the growth of cities, science, and highly advanced technologies.

Before the Agricultural Revolution, people had simple institutions. These were extended families and
50 simple political institutions, such as councils of elders.
As people gathered in larger groups, they needed more
complex institutions. They developed religions. States
needed schools, armies and governments. Today, we
have many different kinds of institutions. They help to
55 organize our culture.

Review Questions

1. List the events that led to the first civilizations.

_____

_____

2. What are two events of the Agricultural Revolution?

_____

_____

✓ Reading Check

What happened because farmers
were able to grow more food than
they needed?

_____

_____

_____

⌖ Target Reading Skill

What invention led to the Industrial
Revolution?

_____

_____

Key Term

institution (in stuh TOO shun) *n.* a custom or organization with
social, educational, or religious purposes

Objectives

1. Learn how people are organized into groups.
2. Look at language.
3. Explore the role of religion.

Target Reading Skill

Understand Sequence Throughout history, things change. You can show a sequence of changes by simply listing the changes. As you read this section, list some of the changes that have happened in societies. Here is an example for you.

Extended family **changed to** nuclear family.

Vocabulary Strategy

Use Context to Clarify Meaning Social studies textbooks often contain words that are new to you. These textbooks have context clues to help you figure out the meanings of words. Context refers to the words and sentences just before and after each new word. The clues can include examples, explanations, or definitions. As you read, use the graphic organizer as a guide to help you find the meaning of new words.

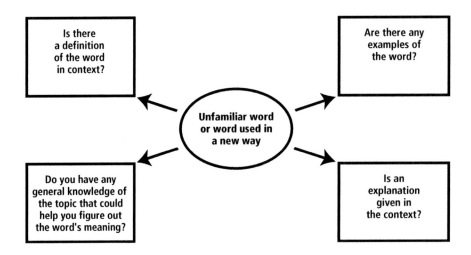

Is there a definition of the word in context?

Are there any examples of the word?

Unfamiliar word or word used in a new way

Do you have any general knowledge of the topic that could help you figure out the word's meaning?

Is an explanation given in the context?

How Society Is Organized

¹ A group of people who share a culture is known as a society. A society may be as small as a single community. Or it may be as large as a nation. It may even be a group of nations. Every society has a social structure.
⁵ Smaller groups in a society work together. For example, teachers, doctors, and farmers are part of the social structure. Social structure helps people work together to meet basic needs.

The family is the basic, most important part of
¹⁰ every society. Families teach the customs and traditions of the culture to their children. ✅

Society is also organized into social classes. A person's place in society may come from wealth, land, ancestors, or education. In the past, it was often hard for people to move from one social class to another. Today, people in many societies can improve their position in society. They can get a good education, make more money, or marry into a higher class.

In some cultures, people think of family as a moth-
²⁰ er, father, and children. The nuclear family is common in the United States.

Other cultures have extended families. In addition to the parents and children, there are the children's wives and husbands. It also includes the children's
²⁵ children. In extended families, older people often help care for the children. They are respected for their knowledge and experience. They pass on traditions. Extended families are not as common as they once were. As people move to cities, nuclear families are
³⁰ becoming more common.

✓ Reading Check

What is the most important part of any society?

_____

_____

Target Reading Skill

In the past, it was hard for people to move from one social class to another. Read the bracketed paragraph to find out if that has changed. Has it? How?

_____

_____

_____

Key Terms

society (suh SY uh tee) *n.* a group of people sharing a culture
social structure (SOH shul STRUK chur) *n.* a pattern of organized relationships among groups of people within a society
social class (SOH shul klas) *n.* a grouping of people based on rank or status
nuclear family (NOO klee ur FAM uh lee) *n.* a mother, a father, and their children
extended family (ek STEN did FAM uh lee) *n.* a family that includes several generations

Language

All cultures have language. Cultures depend on language. People learn their cultures through language. ✓

Language describes the things that are important to that culture. For example, English has words for
35 Christian and Jewish beliefs. Other languages do not have words for these beliefs because their speakers are not Christian or Jewish. But they have words for the beliefs of their religion.

In some countries, people speak more than one lan-
40 guage. Canada has two official languages, English and French. In the United States, you usually hear English, but you can also hear Spanish, Chinese, and other languages. India has 16 official languages, but people there speak more than 800 languages!
45 A country can have more than one culture when its people speak different languages. This is because they may have different festivals or different customs. They talk about different things.

What does the word *ethics* mean? Use the graphic organizer on page 38 to help you figure out what it means. Then write a definition below.

_____

_____

_____

Religion

Religion is another important part of every culture. It helps people make sense of the world. It provides comfort and hope in hard times. It helps answer questions about life and death. And it guides people in <u>ethics</u>, or how to act toward others. People of the same religion may practice their religion differently. ✓
55 Religious beliefs vary. Members of some religions believe in one God. Members of others believe in more than one god. But all religions have prayers and rituals. Every religion celebrates important places and times. All religions expect people to treat one another
60 well and to behave properly.

Review Questions

1. What is the difference between an extended family and a nuclear family?

_____

_____

2. What do all religions expect people to do?

_____

_____

Objectives

1. Explore how cultures change.

2. Learn how ideas spread from one culture to another.

Target Reading Skill

Recognize Words That Signal Sequence Signal words are words or phrases that prepare you for what is coming next. They are like following the directions in a recipe for baking a cake. When baking, you need to pay attention to the order of when ingredients are added, how long to mix or bake, and when to ask an adult to take something out of the oven.

When you read, look for words such as *first, next, then, later, before,* or *at that time.* They signal the order in which the events took place.

Vocabulary Strategy

Use Context to Clarify Meaning Sometimes you may read a word you recognize, but you aren't sure about its meaning. Many words have more than one meaning. What a word means depends on its context. Look for clues in the surrounding words or sentences. For example, the word *matter* has many meanings. You will find what meaning the author had in mind by looking at the context.

Some examples of *matter* are listed in the chart below.

Word	Definitions	Examples
matter	what all things are made of	It was made up of organic matter.
	subject of concern	It was a personal matter.
	material that is spoken or written	This package contains only printed matter.
	trouble	What is the matter?
	to be important	My grades matter to me.

How Cultures Change

All cultures change over time. Just look at the culture of blue jeans. They were invented in the United States. At first, only Americans wore them. But today, jeans are popular all over the world. This culture of clothing changed.

Cultures are always changing. Culture is an entire way of life. A change in one part changes other parts. Changes in the natural environment, technology, and ideas all affect culture.

New technologies change a culture. During the 1800s and early 1900s, industry grew and factories spread. Americans moved from the countryside to the cities. Because people had to walk to work, they had to live close to the factories. Cities grew as a result.

The invention of the car in the late 1800s changed all this. By 1920, many Americans had cars. People could live farther from their jobs and drive to work. The idea of owning a house with a yard became more popular. That led to the growth of suburbs since the mid-1900s. A new culture based on car travel began. ✓

Technology has changed the culture in other ways. Radio and television brought entertainment and news into homes. Today, instant information is part of our culture. Computers change how and where people work. They even help people live longer. Doctors use computers to treat patients.

Cultural change has been going on for a long time. Controlling fire helped people survive colder climates. When people started to farm, they could stay in one place. Before that, they moved about in search of wild plants and animals.

How Ideas Spread

The airplane has made it easier for people to move all over the world. When they move, they bring new kinds of clothing and tools with them. They also bring new ideas.

✓ Reading Check

How did the invention of cars change culture?

_____

_____

_____

⊙ Target Reading Skill

What do the words *Before that*, in the bracketed paragraph, tell you about the sequence of events? Place the events in the paragraph in the order they took place.

1. _____

2. _____

3. _____

Ideas can travel to new places in other ways. People may buy something from another culture then learn to make it themselves. <u>They may learn from other cultures through written matter.</u> This movement of customs and ideas is called cultural diffusion.

Baseball began as an American sport, but today it is played all over the world. That is an example of cultural diffusion. The Japanese love baseball. But they have changed the game to fit their culture. These changes are an example of acculturation. Americans value competition. They focus on winning. A baseball game isn't over until one team wins. In Japan, a game can end in a tie. The Japanese focus on how well the game is played, not on winning.

For thousands of years, cultures changed slowly. People, ideas, and goods moved by foot, or wagon, or boat. Now things go much faster. Faxes and computers send information almost instantly. Magazines and television bring ideas and information from all over the world to any home. When ideas are shared quickly, culture changes quickly. ✓

Change can help, but it can also hurt. If things change too fast, people may feel that they are losing their culture. It is hard to bring back lost traditions. People are working to preserve their own cultures before it is too late. They want to save their artistic traditions, religious beliefs, and wisdom for future generations.

Review Questions

1. How did the car change where people live?

_____

_____

2. List two ways in which ideas travel from one culture to another.

_____

_____

Key Terms

cultural diffusion (KUL chur ul dih FYOO zhun) *n.* the movement of customs and ideas

acculturation (uh kul chur AY shun) *n.* the process of accepting new ideas and fitting them into a culture

Vocabulary Strategy

The word *matter* is used in the underlined sentence. Find it and circle it. How is it used here? Copy the correct definition from the chart at the beginning of this section.

_____

_____

_____

✓ Reading Check

Why do ideas spread faster today?

_____

_____

_____

1. Ideas and ways of doing things are called
   A. environment.
   B. cultural traits.
   C. cultural landscape.
   D. institutions.

2. What is the name for the change from hunting and gathering to growing more food than farmers need?
   A. the Invention of Tools
   B. the Agricultural Revolution
   C. the Development of Civilizations
   D. the Industrial Revolution

3. What is the most important part of every society?
   A. social classes
   B. governments
   C. the family
   D. nations

4. People learn their cultures mainly through
   A. schools.
   B. government.
   C. religion.
   D. language.

5. Which of the following cultural changes is a result of the invention of the car?
   A. the growth of suburbs
   B. the move from the countryside to the nation's cities
   C. the loss of valuable traditions
   D. the speeding up of cultural change

Short Answer Question

Explain how playing baseball in Japan is an example of acculturation.

_____

_____

_____

_____

_____

Objectives

1. Learn about natural resources.
2. Investigate energy.

Target Reading Skill

Identify Main Ideas Good readers look for the main idea of what they read. The main idea is the most important point. It is the one that includes all the other points, or details. Sometimes the main idea is stated in a sentence at the beginning, middle, or end of the paragraph.

The headings in a textbook give you information about the main idea. Think about the headings as you read the section. Try turning headings into questions to help you find the main idea. As you read, ask yourself, "What is this about?"

The first heading on the next page is What Are Natural Resources? Which of the sentences that follow the heading is the main idea? *Hint:* It is the sentence that answers the question that the heading asks.

Vocabulary Strategy

Using Word Origins Many English words are made from Greek roots, or word parts. When scientists need a new word they often use Greek roots.

In this chapter, you will read the word *geothermal*. It is made up of two Greek roots:

geo (from *gaia*, which means *earth*) + *therm* (which means *heat*)

Now that you know its Greek roots, can you figure out what *geothermal* means?

Other English words that are related to these Greek roots are *geography*, and *thermostat*. See if you can answer this. What is the name of the instrument a doctor uses to see how high your temperature is when you have a fever?

What Are Natural Resources?

1 Everything that people use is made with natural resources. Natural resources are things like water, minerals, and plants.

People use some resources just as they are found in
5 nature. Fresh water is one of these. But most resources must be changed first. Resources that must be changed or worked are called raw materials. For example, trees are the raw materials for paper and wood.

The world is filled with natural resources. But not
10 all resources are alike. There are two main groups.

Renewable resources can be replaced. Some are replaced naturally because of the way Earth works. Water is one of these. Earth has a steady supply of water because of the water cycle.

Some types of energy are renewable resources. Solar energy is a renewable resource. No matter how much of the sun's energy we use, there will always be more. The same is true for geothermal energy.

Living things such as plants and animals are also
20 renewable resources. With proper planning, people can have a steady supply of living resources. For example, timber companies can plant new trees to replace the ones they cut down.

The second major group of resources is called non-
25 renewable resources. They include most nonliving things, such as metal ores, most minerals, natural gas, and petroleum. These cannot be replaced. Coal, natural gas, and petroleum are called fossil fuels. Scientists think they were created from the remains of prehistoric
30 living things. In time, these fuels will run out. ✓

Target Reading Skill

Which sentence directly states the main idea of the bracketed paragraph? Circle the sentence.

✓ Reading Check

What is the difference between renewable and nonrenewable resources?

_____

_____

Key Terms

natural resources (NACH ur ul REE sawr siz) *n.* useful materials found in the environment

raw materials (raw muh TIHR ee ulz) *n.* natural resources that must be worked to be useful

renewable resources (rih NOO uh bul REE sawr siz) *n.* natural resources that can be replaced

nonrenewable resources (nahn rih NOO uh bul REE sawr siz) *n.* natural resources that cannot be replaced

---

However, many metals, minerals, and plastics can be recycled. The resource can be reused. The material hasn't been replaced, but recycling means we will use less of the resource.

A Special Resource: Energy

35 Many natural resources are sources of energy. People use energy from fossil fuels. They also use energy from the wind and the sun. Dams use the power of falling water to make hydroelectric power.

People in every country need energy. But energy 40 resources are not spread evenly around the world. Some areas have many energy resources. Others have few.

Countries like Canada and Saudi Arabia have more energy resources than they need. They sell some to 45 other countries. Countries like Japan and the United States cannot make as much energy as they use. They have to buy energy from other countries. ✔

Every day, people use more and more energy. There are not enough fossil fuels to meet energy needs in the 50 future. This means that people will have to find other kinds of energy.

Here are some ideas. Wind and solar energy are available. Geothermal energy is energy from the heat of Earth's interior. It will not run out. Biomass, or plant material, is a renewable source of energy.

Atomic energy uses radioactive materials. They are not renewable, but they are plentiful. Radioactive materials can be dangerous. On the other hand, atomic energy does not pollute the air.

60 Fossil fuels will last longer if people use less energy. New technologies can help. You may have seen hybrid cars. They use less gas. If people use less energy now, there will be more energy in the future.

Review Questions

1. Why are trees considered a renewable resource?

_____

_____

2. List two ways that people can use less energy.

_____

_____

✓ **Reading Check**

Why do some countries have to buy energy?

_____

_____

_____

Vocabulary Strategy

The word *energy* comes from a Greek root that means *work* or *activity*. The bracketed paragraph describes several different kinds of energy. Pick one and write a sentence that describes how that form of energy works for us.

_____

_____

_____

_____

Objectives

1. Study the link between land use and culture.
2. Investigate the link between land use and economic activity.
3. Explore changes in land use.

 **Target Reading Skill**

Identify Supporting Details The main idea of a paragraph or section is its most important point. The main idea is supported by details. Details explain the main idea. They may give additional facts or examples. They can tell you *what, where, why, how much,* or *how many.*

In the second paragraph on the next page, the first sentence states the main idea:

Even in similar environments, people may use land differently.

To find the details, ask yourself, "*How* do people use land differently?"

Vocabulary Strategy

Using Word Origins Many English words came from other languages. For example, many words have been made by combining Latin word parts. In fact, all of the key terms in this section are based on Latin words. We will look at one of them now. You can use a dictionary to find the Latin word parts of the others.

Let's take a closer look at the word *manufacturing*. It is made up of two Latin word parts:

manu ("hand") + *factura* ("making")

To manufacture means to make something by hand. What do you call a place where things are manufactured? *Hint:* The word begins with the Latin word part for *making*.

Land Use and Culture

[1] How people use their land depends on their culture. People may use land differently because their cultures have developed in different environments. The Inuit live in a cold, arctic climate. It is too cold to grow crops. [5] The Inuit use their land mainly for hunting wild animals. The Japanese live in a warmer, wetter climate. Their main crop is rice. It grows well in Japan's climate.

Even in similar environments, people may use land differently. That is because they have different cultural [10] traits. Georgia has a climate like Japan. But farmers in Georgia don't grow rice. Instead, Georgians raise chickens and grow crops like peanuts. The Japanese eat rice at nearly every meal. But Americans eat more meat and peanut butter. ☑

[15] Cultures change landscapes. Thousands of years ago, Western Europe was covered with forests. Then farming cultures began to spread across the region. People cleared forests to use the land for farming. Today, most of the land is open fields and pastures.

[20] Different cultures respond differently to their environments. Much of the western United States has a dry climate. People use pipes and sprinklers to water crops. The Middle East also has a dry climate. But Middle Eastern farmers use qanats, or brick irrigation [25] channels, to water their crops. Both cultures live in similar environments. But they do things differently.

Land Use and Economic Activity

There are three ways of making a living. Geographers have grouped these ways into three stages or levels.

In the first stage, people use land and resources directly to make products. They may hunt, cut wood, mine, or fish. They may herd animals or raise crops. Most of the world's land is used for first-level activities. In developed countries, such as the United States, only a few people make a living in this way. ☑

Key Term

environment (en VY run munt) *n.* natural surroundings

✓ Reading Check

Even though the climate in Georgia is good for growing rice, farmers in Georgia don't grow rice. Why?

_____

_____

_____

◎ Target Reading Skill

List three details in the bracketed paragraph about first-level activities.

1. _____

_____

2. _____

_____

3. _____

_____

✓ Reading Check

How is most of the world's land used?

_____

_____

_____

At the second stage, people process the products of the first-level activities. For example, they turn trees into lumber, or wool from sheep into sweaters. Most second-level activity is manufacturing. Manufacturing is important in developed countries, especially in cities.

40   Third-level activities are also known as services. While services do not produce goods, services may help deliver or sell goods. Many businesses offer services. They include doctors, bankers, automobile repair workers, and clerks. Services are often found in cities, 45 especially in developed countries.

Changes in Land Use

During colonization, the newcomers may change the landscape. If farmers move to an area without farms, they will create farms. As people find new ways of making a living, they will start using the land in new 50 ways, too.

Crops such as wheat and grapes were unknown in the Americas before colonization. So were animals such as cows and chickens. When Europeans came, they cleared large areas for their crops and animals. ☑

55   Since the 1800s, industrialization has changed landscapes in many countries. Cities have grown around factories. Since 1900, suburbs have spread. The spread of cities and suburbs is known as sprawl.

Review Questions

1. What are second-level activities?

_____

_____

2. How are second-level activities different from third-level activities?

_____

_____

Vocabulary Strategy

The word *automobile* combines the Greek word *auto* ("self") and the Latin word *mobile* ("to move").

Try this one yourself. If a biography is the story of someone's life, what is an *autobiography*?

_____

_____

_____

✓ Reading Check

How did European colonization change the American landscape?

_____

_____

_____

Key Terms

manufacturing (man yoo FAK chur ing) *n.* the large-scale production of goods by hand or by machine

colonization (kahl uh nuh ZAY shun) *n.* the movement of settlers and their culture to a new country

industrialization (in dus tree ul ih ZAY shun) *n.* the growth of machine-powered production in an economy

Prepare to Read

Section 3
People's Effect on the Environment

Objectives

1. Investigate how first-level activities affect the environment.
2. Explore how second- and third-level activities affect the environment.

Target Reading Skill

Identify Implied Main Ideas Have you ever had a conversation with someone where you had to pay close attention to what they were saying? Maybe they were telling you all the details about a family event, but what they were actually talking about was how important their family is to them.

Sometimes reading is like that. The main idea is not stated directly. Instead, the details in a paragraph or section add up to a main idea. In a case like this, we say the main idea is implied. It is up to you to put the details together. You will then be able to see the main idea.

For example, the details in the first paragraph on the next page add up to this main idea:

First-level activities are necessary for human survival, but they reshape the environment.

Vocabulary Strategy

Using Word Origins Many English words have been made from Greek word parts. Some of these word parts are names for new inventions. For example, the ancient Greeks used the word part "tele" to mean *far off.* They used the word part "phone" to mean *sound.* We put those word parts together to give us *telephone.* Now that is something the ancient Greeks never imagined!

There are many other words that use each of these roots. Below is a partial list.

telecommunication	telescope
telecommute	television
telegraph	headphone
telemarketing	microphone

First-Level Activities

¹ In first-level activities people use raw materials to get food and resources to live. In the process the environment changes. For example, crops replace wild plants.

As countries grow, new ways of farming are tried. ⁵ In the Great Plains of North America, farms have replaced land where buffalo roamed. In the Netherlands, people have drained wetlands to create dry farmland. Creating new farmland destroyed wild grasslands and wetlands. But the new land has fed ₁₀ millions of people. ✓

Agriculture, forestry, and fishing provide resources that people need to live. But they sometimes hurt the environment. Wood is needed to build houses. But cutting down too many trees can lead to deforestation. ₁₅ Animals that depend on the forest may also suffer. Deforestation can lead to a loss of biodiversity.

Farmers use fertilizers to grow crops. More people can be fed. But rain washes the chemicals into streams. This harms fish and the people who eat the fish.

₂₀ The key is to find a balance. Around the world, people are working to find ways of meeting their needs without hurting the environment. One way is to plant tree farms. Or farmers can use natural methods to grow crops. Or they can use chemicals that will not ₂₅ damage waterways. Fishers can catch fish that are more plentiful.

Second- and Third-Level Activities

Over the years industry, or second-level activities, and services, or third-level activities have changed deserts, prairies, and forests. These activities have created a landscape of cities, factories, offices, highways, and shopping malls.

✓ Reading Check

What is one way people have created new farmland?

_____

_____

_____

Target Reading Skill

In one sentence, state what all the details in the bracketed paragraph are about.

_____

_____

Key Terms

deforestation (dee fawr uh STAY shun) *n.* a loss of forest cover in a region

biodiversity (by oh duh VUR suh tee) *n.* a richness of different kinds of living things in a region

Industrial and service activities provide most of the jobs in developed countries. The main purpose of some of these activities is to change the environment. Civil
35 engineering builds structures that change the landscape. For example, dams create lakes that cover large areas with water. They provide water for farms and cities. They also protect areas from flooding.

Other industrial and service activities have side
40 effects on the environment. Industries use large amounts of resources. They release industrial wastes into the environment. Service activities require the building of roads, telephone lines, and power lines. ✓

Industry is not the only source of pollution. Our
45 own trash may pollute the soil, water, or air. Exhaust from cars and trucks causes air pollution. Air pollution may cause harmful changes in our climate.

Working together, people can find solutions to these problems. One is to use more fuel-efficient cars. Cars
50 that burn less fuel create less air pollution. Renewable energy resources pollute less than fossil fuels.

Waste can be recycled to reduce the amount that must be burned or dumped. It also saves natural resources. For example, paper can be recycled. Then
55 fewer trees have to be cut down to make new paper.

Finding ways to solve environmental problems is one of the greatest challenges of our time.

Review Questions

1. How does deforestation hurt the environment?

_____

_____

2. List ways in which industrial and service activities change landscapes.

_____

_____

✓ Reading Check

How do industrial activities affect the environment?

_____

_____

Vocabulary Strategy

The word *industry* comes from the Latin word *industrius* ("hard working"). What does it mean to say that someone is industrious?

_____

_____

Key Terms

civil engineering (SIV ul en juh NIHR ing) *n.* technology for building structures that alter the landscape, such as dams, roads, and bridges
pollution (puh LOO shun) *n.* waste, usually man-made, that makes the air, water, or soil less clean

1. Resources that must be worked are called
   A. renewable resources.
   B. nonrenewable resources.
   C. recyclable materials.
   D. raw materials.

2. Which of the following is a renewable resource?
   A. water
   B. metal ore
   C. natural gas
   D. coal

3. Manufacturing is an example of
   A. a first-level activity.
   B. a second-level activity.
   C. a third-level activity.
   D. all of the above

4. Cutting down too many trees can lead to
   A. biodiversity.
   B. deforestation.
   C. pollution.
   D. loss of biomass.

5. In developed countries, most of the jobs are in
   A. agriculture.
   B. first-level activities.
   C. industrial and service activities.
   D. first- and third-level activities.

Short Answer Question

List three ways that people affect the environment.

_____

_____

_____

_____

The United States and Canada

CHAPTER 6

Prepare to Read

Section 1 Land and Water

Objectives

1. Learn where the United States and Canada are located.
2. Discover the major landforms of the United States and Canada.
3. Explain how major bodies of water are important to the United States and Canada.

Target Reading Skill

Preview and Set a Purpose Reading a textbook is different from reading a novel or the newspaper. To read effectively, you must preview and set a purpose for your reading.

Before you read this section, take a moment to preview it. Look at the title "Land and Water" and the objectives. Now flip through the next two pages. Read each heading. They tell you about the section's content. They tell you what to expect to learn from each section. As you preview, use this information to give yourself a reason to read the section. Are you curious about anything in the section, like what the land is like in Canada? Read to satisfy that curiosity—that's your purpose for reading.

Vocabulary Strategy

Using Context Clues Words work together to explain meaning. The meaning of a word may depend on its context. A word's context is the other words and sentences that surround it. The context provides clues to a word's meaning.

Try this example. Say that you don't know the meaning of the word *glacier* in the following sentence.

> Large <u>glaciers</u> are found in many mountain ranges in the United States. They are formed when layers of unmelted snow press together, thaw a little, then turn to ice.

You could ask yourself: "What information do the sentences give me about the word?" Answer: "I know that glaciers are formed when layers of unmelted snow press together, and turn to ice. This tells me that glaciers are made of snow and ice." A glacier is a huge, slow-moving chunk of snow and ice.

Section 1 Summary

A Global Perspective

The United States and Canada are both part of North America. The Atlantic Ocean is to the east. The Pacific Ocean is to the west. North of Canada is the Arctic Ocean. South of the United States is Mexico and the Gulf of Mexico. The United States also includes Alaska and Hawaii. ☑

Landforms

The United States and Canada form one landmass. The Rocky Mountains run down the western side of the continent. The Rockies are the largest mountain range in North America. Another major range is the Appalachian (ap uh LAY chun) Mountains in the United States. These mountains meet the Laurentian (law REN shun) Highlands, a mountain range in Canada.

A huge plains area lies between the Rockies and the Appalachians. In Canada, the plains are called the Interior Plains. In the United States, they are called the Great Plains and the Central Plains. This area has rich soil. Another fertile plain, the Gulf-Atlantic Plain, runs along the eastern and southern coasts of the United States. This flat, rich land attracted settlers. ☑

The Great Basin is west of the Rockies. It holds both Death Valley and the Great Salt Lake. There are three more mountain ranges farther west. The Coast Ranges run along the Pacific Ocean, the Sierra Nevada are in California, and the Cascades are in Washington and Oregon. Glaciers are found in some of these mountain ranges. Glaciers are formed when layers of snow press together, thaw a little, then turn to ice.

The Coast Mountains run along the Pacific Ocean in Canada. East of the Interior Plains is the Canadian Shield. This huge region of rock covers about half of Canada. The land is so rugged that few people live there.

Key Terms

Rocky Mountains (RAHK ee MOWN tunz) *n.* the major mountain range in western North America

glacier (GLAY shur) *n.* a huge slow-moving mass of snow and ice

---

✓ **Reading Check**

Which bodies of water border the United States and Canada?

1. _____

2. _____

3. _____

4. _____

✓ **Reading Check**

What large landform lies in both the United States and Canada but is called a different name in each country?

_____

_____

_____

Target Reading Skill

If your purpose is to learn about the geography of Canada, how does the last paragraph on this page help you meet your goal?

_____

_____

_____

Southeast of the Canadian Shield are the St. Lawrence Lowlands. They run along the St. Lawrence River. This is Canada's smallest region. However, more than half the country's people live there. The region is a manufacturing center. Because it contains fertile land, one third of Canada's crops are produced there.

Major Bodies of Water

Both the United States and Canada have many major bodies of water. People use them for transportation, recreation, and industry. The five Great Lakes are Lakes Superior, Michigan, Huron, Erie, and Ontario. Four of the lakes lie on the United States-Canada border. The Great Lakes were formed by glaciers long ago. They are important waterways for both countries. ☑

The largest river in the United States is the Mississippi River. It flows south from Minnesota to the Gulf of Mexico. The Ohio and Missouri rivers are major tributaries of the Mississippi. Today, the Mississippi is one of the busiest waterways in the world.

There are two major rivers in Canada. The Mackenzie River starts in the Rocky Mountains and flows north to the Arctic Ocean. Canada's second major river is the St. Lawrence River. It is one of North America's most important transportation routes. It flows from the Great Lakes to the Atlantic Ocean. It helps trade between the United States and Canada. <u>Locks and canals allow large ships to navigate it.</u>

Review Questions

1. Why do few people live in the Canadian Shield?

_____

_____

2. Name three important rivers in the United States and Canada.

_____

_____

Key Terms

Great Lakes (grayt layks) *n.* the world's largest group of fresh-water lakes

tributary (TRIB yoo tehr ee) *n.* a river or stream that flows into a larger river

Prepare to Read

Section 2 Climate and Vegetation

Objectives

1. Learn what climate zones the United States and Canada have.
2. Identify the natural vegetation zones of the United States and Canada.

Target Reading Skill

Preview and Predict Making predictions about what you will learn from your text helps you set a purpose. It also helps you remember what you have read. Before you begin reading, preview the section. Look at the section title and objectives above, then the headings. Then predict what the section will tell you. Based on your preview, you will probably predict that this section will tell you about the climate and plants of the United States and Canada.

List two facts you expect to learn about climate and plants.

Prediction 1: _____

Prediction 2: _____

As you read, check your predictions. Were they right? If they were not accurate, you may need to pay closer attention when you preview the section.

Vocabulary Strategy

Using Context Clues Sometimes you can pick up clues from the words, phrases, and sentences around an unfamiliar word that will help you understand it. The underlined words in the paragraph below give clues to the meaning of the word *latitude*.

> **Latitude** also affects climates in the United States. <u>Because it is far from the Equator</u>, Alaska is cold for a good part of the year. Hawaii and the southern tip of Florida are <u>much closer to the Equator</u>. Here, it is almost always hot.

The underlined clues told you about where three places are in relation to the Equator. Did the clues help you discover that latitude is a way of measuring distance from the Equator?

Climate Zones

Climate regions in the United States and Canada range from hot deserts to freezing polar regions. There are three things that affect climate: location, oceans, and mountains. ✓

In general, the farther a place is from the Equator, the colder it is. Much of Canada is a long way from the Equator. Therefore, much of Canada is very cold.

The ocean affects climates, too. Water takes longer to heat up or cool down. Being near water helps keep land warm in the winter and cool in the summer. Canada's west coast has a mild climate. Areas far from the ocean often have extreme climates. For example, Canada's Interior Plains have very cold winters and hot summers. Mountains affect climate in a different way. Winds blowing from the Pacific Ocean rise as they meet mountain ranges. As they rise, they cool and drop their moisture. This effect makes Canada's west coast rainy. When the air reaches the other side of the mountains, it is dry. The sheltered side of a mountain is in a rain shadow. This means it receives little rainfall.

Latitude, or distance from the Equator, also affects climates in the United States. Because it is far from the Equator, Alaska is cold for much of the year. Hawaii and the southern tip of Florida are much closer to the Equator. Here, it is almost always hot.

The Pacific Ocean and mountains affect climate in the western United States in a way similar to how the same factors affect Canada's west coast. Wet winds rise up from the ocean and drop their moisture before they cross the mountains. The areas east of the mountains are sheltered from rain and as a result, are very dry.

East of the Great Plains, the United States has continental climates. In the north, summers are warm and winters are cold and snowy. In the south, summers are hot and winters are mild.

Natural Vegetation Zones

There are four major kinds of natural vegetation, or plant life, in the United States and Canada. They are tundra, grassland, desert scrub, and forest.

√ Reading Check

List three factors that affect climate.

1. _____

2. _____

3. _____

Vocabulary Strategy

What does the term *rain shadow* mean in the underlined sentence? What clues can you find in the surrounding words, phrases, or sentences? Circle the words in the paragraph that could help you figure out what *rain shadow* means.

_____

_____

_____

The tundra is a cold, dry region covered with snow for more than half the year. It is found in the far north. The Arctic tundra contains permafrost. Summers are short and cool. Some plants are able to grow during summer. The Inuits (IN oo its) live there. The Inuits are a native people of Canada and Alaska.

Grasslands are regions of flat or rolling land covered with grasses. These grasses grow where there is not enough rain to support forests. In North America, they are called prairies. The world's largest prairie stretches from the American central states into some Canadian provinces. The Canadian provinces of Alberta, Saskatchewan (sus KACH uh wun), and Manitoba are sometimes called the Prairie Provinces.

In desert scrub regions, few plants can grow because there is little water. The Great Basin is one such region. The entire basin is in a rain shadow, between the Rocky Mountains and the Sierra Nevada. Because it is in a rain shadow, it is very dry. It cannot support much life. But sheep graze on the area's short grasses and shrubs.

Forests cover nearly one third of the United States and almost one half of Canada. Some forests are coniferous (koh nif ur us), with trees that make cones to carry their seeds. These forests are filled with pine, fir, and spruce. Other forests have deciduous (dee sij oo us) trees. These trees shed their leaves in the fall. ☑

Review Questions

1. How do oceans influence climate?

_____

_____

2. Where is the largest prairie in the world?

_____

_____

Target Reading Skill

Based on what you've read so far, is your prediction on target? If not, write a new prediction on the lines below.

_____

_____

_____

✓ Reading Check

Name the four major kinds of natural vegetation in the United States and Canada.

1. _____

2. _____

3. _____

4. _____

Key Terms

tundra (TUN druh) *n.* a cold, dry region covered with snow for more than half the year

permafrost (PUR muh frawst) *n.* a permanently frozen layer of ground below the top layer of soil

prairie (PREHR ee) *n.* a region of flat or rolling land covered with tall grasses

province (PRAH vins) *n.* a political division of land in Canada

Objectives

1. Learn about the major resources of the United States.
2. Find out about the major resources of Canada.

Target Reading Skill

Preview and Ask Questions Before you read this section, preview the section titles, objectives, and headings to see what the section is about. What do you think are the most important concepts in the section? How can you tell?

After you preview the section, write two questions that will help you understand or remember important concepts or facts in the section. For example, you might ask yourself:

- Are forests still an important resource?
- Where does Canada get its energy?

Find the answers to your questions as you read.

As you read, keep asking questions about what you think will come next. Does the text answer your questions? Were you able to predict what would be covered under each heading?

Vocabulary Strategy

Using Context Clues Many English words have more than one meaning. You can use context clues to figure out the meaning of these words. For example, in the sentences below, the word *back* is used in two different ways.

He wrote his answers on the <u>back</u> of the worksheet.

Using context clues in this sentence, you can figure out that *back* means "reverse side."

She asked her friends to <u>back</u> her plan.

Using context clues in this sentence, you can figure out that *back* means "support."

Section 3 Summary

Resources of the United States

1 North America is a land of plenty. It has fertile soil, water, forests, wildlife, fuel resources, and minerals. These resources helped make the United States and Canada rich countries.

5 Let's take a look at the resources of the United States. The Midwest and the South have rich, dark soils. Along the Mississippi and other rivers are alluvial soils. These areas with good soil are important for farming. Until the 1900s, many American farms were
10 owned by families. Since then, many farms have been bought by agribusinesses.

Water is an important resource in the United States. People need water to drink and to grow crops. Factories use water. And people use rivers to transport
15 goods. The Mississippi, Ohio, and Missouri rivers are main shipping routes. Water is also used to generate hydroelectricity. ☑

America's forests are also a vital resource. There are forests in the Pacific Northwest, the South, the Appala-
20 chians, and areas around the Great Lakes. They produce lumber, wood pulp for paper, and wood for furniture.

The United States makes and uses more fossil fuels than any other country. Oil, natural gas, and coal are
25 all fossil fuels. Although the United States buys most of its oil from other countries, there are large oil reserves in Alaska. Both coal and natural gas are found in the United States. Natural gas is used to heat many homes. Coal is used by power plants to produce
30 electricity. It is also used to heat and power industrial facilities.

✓ Reading Check

Why is water an important natural resource?

_____

_____

_____

⊙ Target Reading Skill

Ask and answer a question about fossil fuels.

Question:

_____

Answer:

_____

> **Key Terms**
> **alluvial soil** (uh LOO vee ul soyl) *n.* fertile topsoil left by a river after a flood
> **agribusiness** (AG ruh biz niz) *n.* a large company that runs huge farms
> **hydroelectricity** (hy droh ee LEK trih suh tee) *n.* electric power produced by moving water
> **fossil fuel** (FAHS ul FYOO ul) *n.* a fuel formed over millions of years from animal and plant remains

In addition, the United States has valuable deposits of copper, gold, iron ore, and lead. Only a small part of the economy is based on mining. But these minerals are very important to other industries.

Resources of Canada

35 The first European settlers in Canada worked as fur trappers, loggers, fishers, and farmers. Today, very few Canadians earn their living in these ways.

Less than 10 percent of Canada's land is suitable for farming. Most of the farmland is in the Prairie Prov-
40 inces. This region produces most of Canada's wheat and beef. The St. Lawrence Lowlands are another major farming region.

Canada has more lakes than any other country in the world. About 9 percent of the world's fresh water is in
45 Canada. Before the first railroads were built, the only way to reach some parts of the country was by water. Today, the St. Lawrence and Mackenzie rivers are major shipping routes.

Much of Canada's mineral wealth is in the Cana-
50 dian Shield. <u>The region has large deposits of iron, gold, silver, zinc, copper, and uranium</u>. There are also large oil and natural gas deposits in the Prairie Provinces. ✓

The rivers of Quebec Province generate hydroelec-
55 tricity. They produce so much power that some is sold to the United States.

Almost half of Canada's land is covered in forest. Canada is a leading producer of timber products. These products include lumber, paper, plywood, and wood
60 pulp. British Columbia, Quebec, and Ontario produce most of the timber products.

Review Questions

1. What are the major natural resources of the United States?

_____

_____

_____

2. Where is most of Canada's farmland?

_____

_____

_____

Vocabulary Strategy

The word *deposit* has several meanings. It can mean putting money in a bank. It can mean a payment to keep something safe. Or it can mean the place in the earth where minerals collect. Use context clues to find the meaning of *deposit* in the underlined sentence. Then circle the correct meaning above.

✓ Reading Check

What resources are found in the Canadian Shield?

_____

_____

_____

1. Which of the following is a Canadian mountain range?
   A. the Sierra Nevadas
   B. the Appalachians
   C. the Laurentian Highlands
   D. the Cascades

2. Which river flows from the Great Lakes to the Atlantic Ocean?
   A. Mississippi
   B. St. Lawrence
   C. Mackenzie
   D. Missouri

3. Because it is close to the ocean, Canada's west coast has a
   _____ climate.
   A. cold
   B. hot
   C. mild
   D. dry

4. The world's largest _____ stretches from the American
   central states into Canada.
   A. prairie
   B. tundra
   C. desert
   D. forest

5. What happened to family farms in the United States after the 1900s?
   A. They were mined for mineral deposits.
   B. More and more farmland was purchased by family members.
   C. Farmers turned to hydroelectricity for income.
   D. They were bought by agribusinesses.

Short Answer Question
How does the geography of the Canadian Shield affect Canada?

_____

_____

_____

_____

_____

Prepare to Read

Section 1
The Arrival of the Europeans

Objectives

1. Learn who the first Americans were.
2. Discover the effects the arrival of Europeans had on Native Americans.
3. Find out how the United States won its independence from Great Britain.

Target Reading Skill

Reread Have you ever rewound a video you were watching so that you could better understand what was happening in the movie? Rereading is like that. When you read something again it helps you to understand a word or idea you didn't understand the first time.

When you reread, look for connections. Put together the facts that you do understand. See if you can find the main idea. Think about how the idea you don't understand relates to the main idea.

Vocabulary Strategy

Using Context to Clarify Meaning When you come across new words in your text, they are often defined for you. Sometimes the definition appears in a separate sentence. Sometimes there may be a brief definition in the same sentence. Often, the word *or* is used to introduce the definition. Look at the following examples.

<u>indigenous</u>, which means *belonging to and native to a place*

<u>Missionaries</u> are *religious people who want to convert others to their religion.*

<u>indentured servants</u>, or *people who had to work for a period of years to gain freedom*

The underlined words are defined in context. In these examples, the definitions are in italics. Look for definitions in the context as you come across unfamiliar words in your reading.

The First Americans

Many scientists think that Native Americans came to North America from Asia. They believe that this migration took place during the last ice age. At that time, so much water froze that the level of the sea dropped. This made a land bridge between Siberia and Alaska. Hunters followed herds of animals across the land bridge. Over time, the first Americans spread throughout North and South America. Native Americans developed many different ways of life. ☑

The Europeans Arrive

The way of life for indigenous people in the Americas began to change after 1492. That is when Christopher Columbus sailed to North America from Spain.

Spanish settlers followed Columbus. They settled in many parts of the Americas. They often enslaved Native Americans. Thousands died because of harsh working conditions. Spanish missionaries tried to make Native Americans more like Europeans.

Spain became rich from its American colonies. When other countries saw this, they wanted colonies in the Americas, too. The French claimed land along the St. Lawrence and Mississippi rivers. The French traded with Native Americans for fur. Both the French and Spanish brought diseases with them. Many Native Americans died from these diseases.

English colonists also arrived and settled along the Atlantic Coast. They came to start a new life. Some wanted religious freedom. ☑

The first permanent English settlement was Jamestown, Virginia. It was founded in 1607. In 1619, the first Africans arrived as indentured servants. Later, Africans were brought as slaves. Many were forced to work on large farms in the South.

✓ Reading Check

How did migrating people reach North America?

_____

_____

_____

✓ Reading Check

Name one reason why English settlers came to the Americas.

_____

_____

_____

Key Terms

indigenous (in DIJ uh nus) *adj.* belonging to a certain place
missionary (MISH un ehr ee) *n.* a person who tries to convert others to his or her religion
indentured servant (in DEN churd SUR vunt) *n.* a person who must work for a period of years to gain freedom

In 1620, the Pilgrims arrived in Massachusetts from England. They wanted to worship God in their own way. About 60 years later, William Penn founded the Pennsylvania Colony. He wanted a place where all people were treated fairly.

In 1754, Britain and France went to war over land in North America. The British fought the French and their Native American allies. Americans call this war the French and Indian War. With the colonists' help, the British won in 1763.

The Break with Britain

The British wanted the colonists to help pay for the British army. They put taxes on goods the colonists bought from Britain. The colonists felt this was not fair. The colonists were not represented in Parliament, so they could not protest these taxes. Instead, the colonists boycotted, or refused to buy, British goods.

The colonists rebelled against British rule. They fought the British in the Revolutionary War. After the colonists won independence, the 13 colonies agreed on a plan of government called the Articles of Confederation. But in this plan, Congress was not given the power to tax. Later, the colonies agreed to form a stronger central government. They wrote the Constitution. It is still the highest law of the United States. ✓

Review Questions

1. Where do many scientists believe the first Americans came from?

_____

_____

_____

2. The colonists thought the British taxes were not fair. Why didn't the colonists protest?

_____

_____

_____

> **Key Term**
> **boycott** (boy kaht) *n.* a refusal to buy or use goods and services

Target Reading Skill

Reread the bracketed paragraph to see who fought in the French and Indian War.

_____

_____

_____

Vocabulary Strategy

The term *boycotted* is defined in context. Circle its definition.

✓ Reading Check

What was the problem with the Articles of Confederation?

_____

_____

_____

Prepare to Read

Section 2
Growth and Conflict in the United States

Objectives

1. Explore the effects of westward expansion in the United States.
2. Discover the causes and effects of the Civil War.

Target Reading Skill

Read Ahead Reading ahead can help you understand something you are not sure of in the text. If you do not understand a certain word or passage, keep reading. The word or idea may be explained later on. Sometimes a word is defined after it has been used. The main idea of one paragraph may be discussed in later paragraphs.

When you read the first paragraph of this section, you may not understand what the Louisiana Purchase is. By reading ahead you will find out that it was the sale of land that doubled the size of the United States.

Vocabulary Strategy

Using Context to Clarify Meaning Social studies texts often contain unfamiliar words. To figure out the meaning of a word, look at its context for clues. Context refers to the words, sentences, and paragraphs just before and after the word. As you read, use the graphic organizer as a guide to help you figure out the meaning of unfamiliar or confusing words.

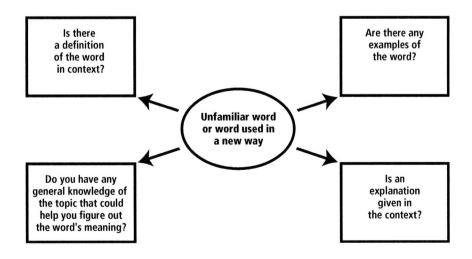

Is there a definition of the word in context?

Are there any examples of the word?

Unfamiliar word or word used in a new way

Do you have any general knowledge of the topic that could help you figure out the word's meaning?

Is an explanation given in the context?

A Nation Grows

1 The United States was not always as large as it is today. The Louisiana Purchase was an important part of America's growth. The Louisiana Territory was originally owned by France. In 1803, France sold the land to 5 the United States for $15 million. The sale included all the land between the Mississippi River and the Rocky Mountains. It doubled the size of the United States.

As the country grew, so did democracy. At first, only white men who owned property could vote. Later, 10 all white men could vote, even if they did not have property. Women, African Americans, and Native Americans, however, could not vote.

For a long time, Native Americans struggled to keep their land. American settlers wanted Native American 15 lands in the southeast. Then in 1830, Congress passed the Indian Removal Act. It forced Native Americans to leave their homelands and move to present-day Oklahoma. ✓

Many people thought that all the land from the Atlantic to the Pacific should belong to the United States. This 20 belief was called Manifest Destiny. Wagon trains with settlers began heading west. In 1845, Texas became part of the United States. After a war with Mexico, the United States won much of what is now the Southwest region.

At the same time, thousands of people were pouring 25 into cities in the Northeast. Some left farms to work in factories. Others were immigrants from Europe. They looked for jobs created by the Industrial Revolution. The Industrial Revolution changed the lives of Americans. New machines made goods much more quickly 30 than they could be made by hand. Other inventions made travel easier and faster.

<hr>

✓ Reading Check

What did the Indian Removal Act do?

_____

_____

_____

<hr>

Key Terms

Louisiana Purchase (loo ee zee AN uh PUR chus) *n.* the sale of land in North America in 1803 by France to the United States
immigrant (IM uh grunt) *n.* a person who moves to a new country in order to settle there
Industrial Revolution (in DUS tree ul rev uh LOO shun) *n.* the change from making goods by hand to making them by machine

The Civil War and Reconstruction

Cotton was an important crop in America in the 1800s. With the Industrial Revolution, the demand for cotton grew. It took many people to grow cotton, so slaves were important. Cotton farmers wanted to expand into western lands, and they wanted slavery there, too. This led to an important question: Who would decide if there was going to be slavery in the growing country?

The debate over slavery kept growing. Most southerners were for slavery. However, thousands of Northerners became abolitionists. Many helped slaves escape to Canada, where slavery was illegal.

Abraham Lincoln, a Northerner, was elected President in 1860. Many Southerners felt they would have little say in the government. Some Southern states seceded, or withdrew, from the United States. They founded a new country. It was called the Confederate States of America, or the Confederacy. The North was known as the Union. ✓

In 1861, the Civil War broke out between the Union and the Confederacy. In 1863, Lincoln issued the Emancipation Proclamation. It declared slaves in the Confederacy to be free. The Union won the Civil War in 1865. Less than a week later, Lincoln was killed. His vice president, Andrew Jackson, tried to carry out Lincoln's plan for Reconstruction. But Congress resisted. It sent the Union Army to control the South. Finally, in 1877, the Union Army withdrew. Southern lawmakers soon voted to segregate blacks from whites. The United States was still one country. But the struggle for equality lay ahead.

Review Questions

1. How did the United States increase its land?

_____

_____

2. Why did people move to Northeastern cities?

_____

_____

Key Terms

abolitionist (ab uh LISH un ist) *n.* a person who believed that enslaving people was wrong and who wanted to end the practice
segregate (SEG ruh gayt) *v.* to set apart, typically because of race or religion

---

Target Reading Skill

Keep reading to see how slavery affected the nation's history. What did you find out?

_____

_____

_____

Vocabulary Strategy

What do you think the word *secede* means in the bracketed paragraph? Use context clues to help you write a definition of the word. Circle words or phrases in the text that helped you write your definition.

_____

_____

_____

✓ Reading Check

Why did some Southern states secede from the United States?

_____

_____

_____

CHAPTER 7

Prepare to Read

Section 3
The U.S. on the Brink of Change

Objectives

1. Explore what happened in the United States from 1865 to 1914.
2. Find out what happened during the World Wars.
3. Explore the challenges the United States faces at home and abroad.

Target Reading Skill

Paraphrase When you paraphrase, you put something into your own words. Putting ideas in your own words will help you remember what you have read.

For example, look at the second paragraph on the next page. You might paraphrase that paragraph by saying:

People moved to the Midwest to escape poverty. The Homestead Act of 1862 gave them land if they farmed it for five years. It was hard work. Most settlers stayed the full five years.

As you read on, paraphrase the information following each heading. Use as few words as possible.

Vocabulary Strategy

Using Context to Clarify Meaning When you come across an unfamiliar word while reading, look for context clues to help you figure out what it means. It is also helpful to consider the topic of the paragraph when you think about the context. The chart below shows how to use clues to determine meaning.

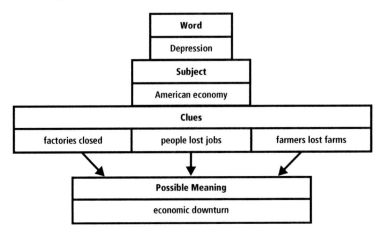

Word
Depression

Subject
American economy

Clues		
factories closed	people lost jobs	farmers lost farms

Possible Meaning
economic downturn

Section 3 Summary

From 1865 to 1914

The Industrial Revolution made life easier for the rich and the middle class. But life did not get better for the poor. City slums were crowded with poor immigrants. They made up a huge labor force, but employers paid them very little.

Some people tried to leave poverty behind by moving to the Midwest. The Homestead Act of 1862 gave land to any adult who would farm it for five years. Life was hard, but most settlers held on for five years. Railroads helped to speed up settlement.

The United States continued to grow. In 1867, the United States bought Alaska from Russia. Then in 1898, the United States took control of Hawaii. The same year, the United States took control of Puerto Rico, Guam, and the Philippines. ✓

The World at War

The United States and World War I

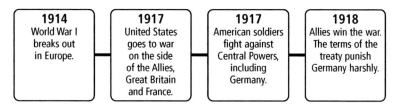

1914	1917	1917	1918
World War I breaks out in Europe.	United States goes to war on the side of the Allies, Great Britain and France.	American soldiers fight against Central Powers, including Germany.	Allies win the war. The terms of the treaty punish Germany harshly.

For 10 years after the war, the American economy boomed. Women were given the right to vote. People bought cars and modern appliances. Then in 1929, the world entered the Great Depression. In America, factories closed, and people lost their jobs, farms, and all their savings.

The Great Depression was very hard on Germany. Adolf Hitler became dictator there. He promised to bring back Germany's wealth and power. Hitler began World War II.

Key Term

labor force (LAY bur fawrs) *n.* the supply of workers

✓ **Reading Check**

How did the United States get Alaska?

_____

_____

_____

Target Reading Skill

Paraphrase the bracketed paragraph in 25 words or less.

_____

_____

_____

The word *ally* is underlined. Use context clues to help you figure out what the word means. Find those clues and circle them.

✓ Reading Check

What led the United States to take part in World War II?

_____

_____

_____

✓ Reading Check

List the two countries involved in the Cold War.

1. _____

2. _____

Japan was an <u>ally</u> of Germany. When Japan attacked the U.S. naval base at Pearl Harbor, Hawaii, the United States entered the war against Germany and Japan. ✓

In 1945, the Allies defeated Germany. Then the United States dropped two atomic bombs on Japan, ending the war. The world soon learned of the horrible mass murder called the Holocaust.

The U.S. at Home and Abroad

After World War II, the United States was a superpower. It faced new challenges at home and in other countries. After the war, the Soviet Union took control of many Eastern European countries. The United States feared that the Soviets were trying to spread communism all over the world. The result was the Cold War, between the United States and the Soviet Union. No actual war took place. The Cold War lasted about 40 years. ✓

The U.S. economy boomed after World War II, but not all citizens shared the benefits. Many African Americans still faced racial discrimination. They sought their civil rights. They were led by people like Martin Luther King, Jr. The movement's success inspired other groups.

New challenges face America. On September 11, 2001, terrorists attacked New York City and Washington, D.C. In response to attacks like these, the United States took military action in Afghanistan and Iraq. It was also meant to prevent future terrorist attacks.

Review Questions

1. Who did not benefit from the Industrial Revolution?

_____

_____

2. Who fought for civil rights after World War II?

_____

_____

Key Terms

Holocaust (HAHL uh kawst) *n.* the murder of six million Jews during World War II

Cold War (kohld wawr) *n.* a period of great tension between the United States and the Soviet Union

civil rights (SIV ul ryts) *n.* the basic rights due to all citizens

terrorist (TEHR ur ist) *n.* a person who uses violence and fear to achieve goals

Objectives

1. Learn about why France and Britain were rivals in Canada.
2. Discover how Canada became an independent nation.
3. Explore how Canada became a world power in the 1900s.

Target Reading Skill

Summarize A good summary includes important events and details. It notes the order of events and the connections among events or details.

As you read the next two pages, use a table like the one below to list key events and details. This will help you summarize the history of Canada. Under each heading, write the key points that you think are important. For example, under "The French and British," you could write: "conflict over fur trade in Canada led to treaty in 1713."

Listing all the key points will make summarizing easier.

The History of Canada

The French and the British	Canada Seeks Independence	Postwar to Present

Vocabulary Strategy

Using Context to Clarify Meaning When you come across a word that you do not know, you may not need to look it up in a dictionary. In this workbook, key terms appear in blue. The definitions are in a box at the bottom of the page. Looking at the definition may break up your reading. Before you do that, continue to read to the end of the paragraph. See if you can figure out what the word means from its context. Clues can include examples and explanations. Then look at the definition on the bottom of the page to see how accurate you were. Finally, reread the paragraph to make sure you understand what you read.

The French and the British

1 The fur trade in Canada caused conflict between France and Great Britain. They signed a peace treaty in 1713. The treaty gave Britain the Hudson Bay region, Newfoundland, and part of Acadia. But peace was uneasy.
5 Both France and Britain wanted more control.

This led to the Seven Years' War. Great Britain won the war and got complete control over Canada. Many French settlers left. Those who stayed kept their own language, religion, and customs.

10 During the American Revolution against the British, some Americans did not want independence. They were called Loyalists. After the war, many Loyalists moved to Canada. To avoid problems between French people and people loyal to Britain, Great Britain divided Canada
15 into two colonies. Most Loyalists moved into Upper Canada, now Ontario. French Canadians remained in Lower Canada, which is now Quebec. ✓

Canada Seeks Independence

French Canadians and British Canadians wanted to be free of British rule. Both groups organized separate
20 rebellions. The British defeated both. The British tried to stop the rebellions by uniting Upper and Lower Canada. Some other provinces were not included. The British were afraid a rebellion would be successful if Canada were completely united. ✓

But Canadians wanted all the provinces to be united. In 1864, leaders from every province met. They worked out a plan to form a union. It was accepted by the British Parliament in 1867. The British North American Act made Canada a dominion. It was not completely independent. But Canadians could elect their own leaders and have a central government.

> **Key Term**
> **dominion** (duh MIN yun) *n.* a self-governing area

✓ Reading Check

Why was Canada divided into two colonies?

_____

_____

_____

✓ Reading Check

Why didn't the British want Canada to be united?

_____

_____

_____

Vocabulary Strategy

In the bracketed paragraph, the word *dominion* is a Key Term. Could you figure out its meaning without looking at the definition? Circle the context clues in the paragraph that help you. Then write a definition in your own words.

_____

_____

_____

In the following years, Canada grew and changed. European farmers settled Canada's western plains. Gold and other valuable minerals were found in the Yukon. Canada was becoming rich and important.

During World War I, Canadians were still British subjects. When Britain entered the War, so did Canada. Canada sent soldiers and resources overseas. Canada helped in the World War I victory. As a result, Canada became a world power.

Canada: Postwar to the Present

During World War II, Canadians built factories. They made war supplies and other goods. Immigrants poured into Canada. They filled jobs in new factories and other businesses. Canada became an important
45 industrial nation.

Industrialization brought back old arguments. British Canadians built new factories in Quebec. That alarmed French Canadians. In 1969, new laws made Canada bilingual. However, many people in Quebec
50 still feel that Quebec should be independent.

In 1982, Canada adopted a new constitution. The new constitution made it completely independent from Great Britain. Canada's government is modeled on the British parliamentary system. The government is
55 headed by a prime minister. A group of representatives makes its laws. Canada is also part of the Commonwealth of Nations. The members are all former colonies of Great Britain. They work together on economic issues. ☑

Review Questions

1. What two countries fought over Canada?

_____

_____

2. What do members of the Commonwealth of Nations have in common?

_____

_____

Key Term

bilingual (by LIN gwul) *adj.* having two official languages

Target Reading Skill

Summarize the bracketed paragraphs. Be sure to include the way Canada became a world power.

_____

_____

_____

✓ Reading Check

When did Canadians adopt a new constitution?

_____

_____

_____

Objectives

1. Identify the environmental concerns the United States and Canada share today.
2. Find out about the economic ties the United States and Canada have to each other and to the world.

Target Reading Skill

Reread or Read Ahead Both rereading and reading ahead can help you understand words and ideas in the text. If you do not understand a word or passage, use one or both of these skills to help you.

In some cases, you may wish to read ahead first to see if the word is defined after its first use in a text. By reading ahead you may find that what you do not understand is discussed later in the section.

If you do not understand the main idea of a sentence or paragraph, try going back and rereading it.

Vocabulary Strategy

Using Context to Clarify Meaning Most words have more than one meaning. What a word means will depend on its context. Look for clues in the surrounding words, sentences, or paragraphs. For example, the word *lock* has many meanings. You cannot know what meaning the author had in mind unless you look at the context.

Some of the most common meanings of *lock* are listed in the chart below. The chart also has examples in context.

Word	Definitions	Examples
lock	a mechanical device for keeping something shut	The key is in the lock.
	an enclosed section of a canal with gates at each end	There are several locks in the Panama Canal.
	a length or curl of hair	She gave him a lock of hair.
	to fasten with a lock	Lock the door when you go out.
	to join together firmly	The elks locked horns.

Section 5 Summary

Environmental Issues

The United States and Canada share many geographic features. They share the Atlantic and Pacific coasts. They also share the Great Lakes and the Rocky Mountains. Both countries use natural resources in similar ways. Both use technology to meet their needs. This has affected their water, air, forests, and futures.

In 1969, the Cuyahoga River (ky uh HOH guh RIV er) was so polluted it caught on fire. The Cuyahoga empties into Lake Erie. Lake Erie was so polluted that most of the fish had died. The fire on the Cuyahoga was a wake-up call. The United States and Canada agreed to clean up the lake.

The air in most big cities is filled with a haze of pollution. This haze is caused by cars and factories burning fossil fuels. The air is unhealthy to breathe. It also causes problems miles away. It mixes with moisture to form acid rain. Acid rain kills plants, trees, and fish. Acid rain caused by United States power plants affects forests and lakes in Canada. The Canadian government complained to the United States. The two countries are trying to reduce acid rain.

Many people believe that cutting down trees harms the environment. Logging companies often cut down all the trees in an area. Without trees, soil washes away. Other plants die, and animals lose their homes. But people need to use wood. People who work for logging companies need their jobs. The Canadian and American governments want to support both the forests and the timber industry. They are working on new ways to do both. ✓

Key Term

acid rain (AS id rayn) *n.* rain containing acids that are harmful to plants and trees

Target Reading Skill

Reread or keep reading to see what environmental problems Canada and the United States face.

✓ Reading Check

Name some advantages and disadvantages to logging in forests.

Advantages:

_____

_____

Disadvantages:

_____

_____

"Economics Has Made Us Partners"

Canada and the United States share a very long border. Being economic partners has helped both countries. Part of this cooperation has been in transportation. This is especially true around the Great Lakes.

Lake Superior is at a much higher elevation than the St. Lawrence River, making it impossible to ship goods from the Great Lakes to the Atlantic. To work around this problem, the United States and Canada built the St. Lawrence Seaway. The St. Lawrence Seaway is a system of locks, canals, and dams. The Seaway opened in 1959. Ships can now travel between the Great Lakes and the Atlantic Ocean. The St. Lawrence Seaway makes it much easier for the two countries to trade with each other and with Europe.

45 The United States and Canada are each other's biggest trading partners. Each country needs to do business with the other to be successful. Since 1988, both countries have signed two important free trade agreements. The Free Trade Agreement (FTA) ended tariffs. Tariffs 50 raise the cost of goods, which can limit trade. In 1994, the North American Free Trade Agreement (NAFTA) added Mexico to the agreement. This helps all three countries work together to keep their businesses strong.

Countries need each other in many ways. Both Can-55 ada and the United States belong to the Organization of American States, or OAS. This group of countries works together to keep peace in the Western Hemisphere. ✓

Review Questions

1. What are some environmental problems the United States and Canada share?

_____

_____

2. What does NAFTA do for its member countries?

_____

_____

Key Terms

free trade (free trayd) *n.* trade without taxes on imported goods

tariff (TAR if) *n.* a fee charged on imported goods

Vocabulary Strategy

The word *locks* is used in the bracketed paragraph. Find it and circle it. How is it used here? Copy the correct definition from the chart at the beginning of this section.

_____

_____

_____

✓ Reading Check

What is the purpose of the Organization of American States?

_____

_____

_____

1. Where do scientists think Native Americans originally came from?
   A. North America
   B. South America
   C. Europe
   D. Asia

2. Which event encouraged immigrants and farm workers to look for jobs in cities?
   A. the Louisiana Purchase
   B. the Indian Removal Act
   C. the Industrial Revolution
   D. the Civil War

3. World War I began in Europe in 1914 and ended in _____ when the _____ won.
   A. Pearl Harbor, Central Powers
   B. 1917, Turkey
   C. 1918, Allies
   D. the United States, Allies

4. Canada's help in the World War I victory helped Canada become
   A. a British colony.
   B. a world power.
   C. a French colony.
   D. involved in the War of 1812.

5. What allows ships to travel between the Great Lakes and the Atlantic Ocean?
   A. St. Lawrence Seaway
   B. Cuyahoga River
   C. Panama Canal
   D. Mississippi River

Short Answer Question

Why do the United States and Canada cooperate on environmental problems?

_____

_____

_____

_____

Section 1
A Heritage of Diversity and Exchange

Objectives

1. Explain how cultural patterns developed in the United States and Canada.
2. Discuss what cultural patterns exist today in the United States and Canada.

Target Reading Skill

Identify Main Ideas Good readers are able to find the main idea of what they read. The main idea is the most important point.

To find the main idea of a paragraph, read the paragraph through once. Then ask yourself what the paragraph is about. Do all the sentences center on the same point? If so, you've found your main idea. The main idea of the paragraph below is underlined in blue.

The United States and Canada have similar cultural patterns. They were both once British colonies. Both countries are wealthy, powerful nations. And they both have stable governments.

Vocabulary Strategy

Recognizing Signal Words When playing a video or computer game, you usually have to go through a series of steps to get to the next level. Let's say that your friend was having trouble getting to the next level. If you were to explain to your friend how you got from one level to another, you might use words like *first, next, then, finally, before, afterward, earlier,* and *later.*

These are signal words. There are different kinds of signal words, but the ones above are used to show sequence. They tell you the order of events, or the next step to take. Look for sequence signal words as you read. They will help you remember what you read.

Section 1 Summary

Patterns of Culture Develop

Cultural diversity has long been part of the United States and Canada. Native Americans, European settlers, and immigrants have all contributed to the variety of culture. Both countries are also geographically diverse. They have many different landforms, climates, and plants. Native Americans developed cultures based on their environments. Those near the sea fished. Native Americans living in forests hunted. They also traded with each other. When groups trade, they get more than goods. They also trade ideas. This is called cultural exchange.

The arrival of Europeans changed Native American life. For example, before the Europeans arrived, there were no horses in the Americas. Then the Spanish brought horses with them. Horses became an important part of Native American life. Cultural exchange went both ways. Native Americans contributed to European culture. From the Native Americans, the French and English learned to trap animals and grow corn and pumpkins. Enslaved Africans also contributed to the exchange. ☑

This give-and-take happens whenever immigrants come to a country. Many ethnic groups have made important contributions to American and Canadian cultures.

Cultural Patterns Today

The United States and Canada have similar cultural patterns. That is because they were both once British colonies. Immigration has had an impact on both countries. Today, they are wealthy, powerful nations with stable governments. Immigrants still come to them to improve their lives.

Key Terms

cultural diversity (KUL chur ul duh VUR suh tee) *n.* a variety of cultures

cultural exchange (KUL chur ul eks CHAYNJ) *n.* the process by which different cultures share ideas and ways of doing things

ethnic group (ETH nik groop) *n.* a group of people who share a common language, history, and culture

---

Vocabulary Strategy

Look at the underlined sentences. The events they describe are out of order. However, signal words help show the sequence of events. Rewrite the events in the order in which they occurred.

_____

_____

_____

_____

_____

_____

✓ Reading Check

What are two examples of cultural exchange?

1. _____

_____

2. _____

_____

Many immigrants hold on to things that remind them of their old homes. When immigrants move to a new country, they have to make hard choices. They often learn the country's language and customs to fit in. But many immigrants also want to keep some of the customs of their home culture. Many large cities in the United States and Canada have places where certain ethnic groups live or work. They maintain their traditions and customs. They also enrich life in the United States and Canada.

Few countries in the world are as important to each other as the United States and Canada. They share a common language, border, continent, and history. Their people are very much alike. At least three quarters of the people in both countries live in cities. Canadians and Americans dress alike. They eat the same kinds of food. They practice similar religions. They often enjoy the same movies and sports. Both countries have a high standard of living. ✓

These two countries also need each other for trade. Americans buy Canadian products. Canadians buy American products. The total amount of trade between them is greater than between any other two countries. In addition, millions of Canadians visit the United States each year, while most of Canada's tourists are American.

Review Questions

1. How did the arrival of the Europeans affect Native American culture?

_____

_____

_____

2. Describe trade between the United States and Canada.

_____

_____

_____

Target Reading Skill

Which sentence in the bracketed paragraph states the main idea? Find and underline it.

✓ Reading Check

List three ways that Americans and Canadians are alike.

1. _____

_____

2. _____

_____

3. _____

_____

Prepare to Read

Section 2
The United States: A Nation of Immigrants

Objectives

1. Learn about the people of the United States.
2. Find out what the culture of the United States is like.

Target Reading Skill

Identify Supporting Details The main idea of a paragraph or section is supported by details. Details give more information about the main idea. They give additional facts and examples. They tell you *what, where, why, how much,* or *how many.*

The main idea of the section titled: "The People of the United States" is stated in this sentence: "Americans are a diverse mix of races and religions." As you read, look for details that tell you more about the people of the United States and how diverse they are. Try to find at least three details to support the main idea.

Vocabulary Strategy

Recognizing Signal Words Sometimes when one thing happens, it causes something else to happen. For example, when your alarm doesn't go off in the morning, you don't wake up in time. The cause is the broken alarm clock; the effect is getting up late for school. Cause and effect is easy to see when it happens to you, but it can be harder to see when you are reading. That is why you should look for cause and effect signal words. They tell you that one event or fact is linked to another event or fact.

Some signal words that show cause and effect are:

Cause	Effect
because	as a result
if	so
on account of	then
since	therefore

The People of the United States

1 The population of the United States has grown steadily since 1790. That is when the first national census was taken. About four million people lived in the nation then. Today, more than 280 million people live in the

5 United States. They share many attitudes and traditions. These experiences help bring them together. Americans are a diverse mix of races and religions.

The first people in the United States were Native Americans. <u>They often fought with European settlers</u>

10 <u>over land. The United States government supported white settlement. Therefore, the government forced Native Americans to leave their land and live on reservations.</u> The United States government signed hundreds of treaties with American Indian groups.

15 Native Americans agreed to give up much of their land. In return, the federal government promised to pay for the land and protect them. Many of the treaties were broken by settlers. Native Americans fought over 1,000 battles for their way of life in the late 1800s.

20 In the 1960s, Native Americans began to seek equality. Groups like the American Indian Movement (AIM) worked for better living conditions and equal rights.

The United States has always been a nation of immigrants. A major wave of immigrants came from 1830 to 1890. These people came from England, Scotland, Ireland, Scandinavia, and Germany to farm the land. Because they were like the original European settlers, they fit in easily. However, immigrants from China had a harder time. They came for the California Gold Rush and to lay track for a railroad. They experienced violence and discrimination.

Key Terms

reservation (rez ur VAY shun) *n.* an area of land set aside for a special purpose
treaty (TREE tee) *n.* a formal agreement

Vocabulary Strategy

As you read the underlined sentences, look for cause and effect. Circle the cause and effect signal word when you find it. Then write the cause and effect on the lines below.

Cause:

_____

_____

Effect:

_____

_____

A second wave of immigrants came from 1880 to 1920. These immigrants worked in factories, mills, and mines. Most of them came from southern and eastern Europe. They included many Jews and Roman Catholics. Like the Chinese before them, they dressed differently, ate different foods, and spoke different languages.

40 Today, most immigrants to the United States are from Asia and Latin America. Immigrants have helped the United States develop in many ways. They have helped agriculture, industry, and the economy. They have helped create a culturally diverse nation. ☑

United States Culture

Have you ever eaten bagels, tacos, or spaghetti? A wide variety of foods, books, music, and sports have been 45 added to American culture from other countries. This is the result of the variety of people who live here.

Today, American literature includes works by Latino authors, African-American authors, and Native American authors. This diversity reflects the diversity of the 50 United States.

Americans listen to and record many kinds of music. Jazz is a type of music that was influenced by music from Africa. Like jazz, rock-and-roll began in the United States. It then spread all over the world. Other 55 musical styles enjoyed by Americans include rap, reggae, country, techno, and hip-hop.

Many Americans play or watch sports. Sports began in North America with Native American groups. More recently, three major sports were invented in the United 60 States. They are baseball, basketball, and football. ☑

Review Questions

1. What happened when settlers wanted Native American land?

_____

_____

_____

2. Describe some types of traditions from other countries that have been added to American culture.

_____

_____

_____

Look at the bracketed paragraphs on this page and the previous page. Find three details that support the idea that America is a diverse nation. Underline each one.

✓ Reading Check

Where are most immigrants to the United States today from?

_____

_____

_____

✓ Reading Check

Which major sports were invented in the United States?

_____

_____

_____

Prepare to Read

Section 3 The Canadian Mosaic

Objectives

1. Find out about the people of Canada.
2. Learn about Canadian culture.

Target Reading Skill

Identify Main Ideas How can you find the main idea if it is not stated directly? Sometimes as a reader you have to work a little harder to find out what the main idea is. Sometimes it is up to you to put all the details together and come up with the main idea.

Let's say you just finished reading the paragraphs under the heading "The People of Canada" and you noted that the main idea was not stated. Use the section title, headings, and a chart like the one below to find the main idea.

The People of Canada
Details: 1. 2. 3.
Main Idea:

Vocabulary Strategy

Recognizing Signal Words Sometimes the best way to describe something is to contrast it with something different. Here is an example:

You can drive across Rhode Island in half a day. On the other hand, it takes two days to drive from the northern border of California to the southern border of California.

From these two sentences, you learn that Rhode Island is much smaller than California. The sentences contrast the two states. The signal words that let you know there is a contrast are *on the other hand*.

Other signal words that show contrast include:

although	not	however	despite
but	even though	yet	instead

Section 3 Summary

The People of Canada

Canada has a population of more than 31 million people. Many who live there are immigrants. Canada's leaders used to set limits on immigrants who were not European Christians. Today, people of all ethnic groups move to Canada.

One difference between Canada and the United States is how immigration is viewed. The United States considers itself a melting pot, where cultures blend together. Canada is more like a mosaic, where cultures remain distinct but form a beautiful pattern together.

French Canadians are an example. French Canadians in Quebec want to preserve their heritage. Special laws there promote French culture and language. All signs are written in French, with an English translation below. But many French Canadians want Quebec to become a separate country.

Canada's indigenous peoples are called First Nations. They also want to preserve their culture. However, most of them do not want to be independent. Instead, they are trying to fix past problems. As in the United States, early European settlers in Canada took over the native peoples' lands. Many indigenous people were sent to reserves. Others were denied equal rights. Recent laws allow First Nations to use their own languages in their schools.

Canada's Inuits (IN oo itz) are also trying to improve their lives. Traditionally, they were nomadic hunters and gatherers. For centuries, they lived in the Arctic. They made everything they needed. Modern technology allows them to buy the clothes and tools they used to make. As the Inuits lose traditional skills, they feel they are losing their identity. ✓

Vocabulary Strategy

In the bracketed paragraph, signal words are used to show contrast. Find the signal words and circle them.

✓ Reading Check

How has technology changed the way that Inuits live?

_____

_____

_____

Key Terms

melting pot (MELT ing paht) *n.* a country in which many cultures blend together to form a single culture

reserve (rih ZURV) *n.* an area of land set aside by the government

List three details that support the main idea of the bracketed paragraph. *Hint:* You will need to find the implied main idea first.

1. _____

_____

2. _____

_____

3. _____

_____

Britain and France were the first countries to colonize Canada. By the late 1800s, most Canadians were of British or French descent. By the 1920s, immigrants from central and eastern Europe came. They farmed the prairies in the west. During the Depression, the government limited the number of immigrants. After World War II, the economy grew again. More workers were needed. Millions of immigrants came to Canada. Many were from Africa, Asia, and Latin America. They settled in cities. Since World War II, Canada's population has doubled. Much of that growth is because of immigrants and their children.

Canadian Culture

45   Canada encourages people to be Canadian and still express their ethnic heritage. Canadians are not united by one culture. But there is one thing that most Canadians feel strongly about. They feel that the United States has too much influence on their culture. They look for
50   ways to express their unique culture.

Canadian writers such as Lucy Maud Montgomery and Alice Munro have made Canadian literature popular around the world. Canadian singers such as Shania Twain and Céline Dion have made contributions to
55   cultural life. The Canadian recording industry is a billion dollar business. Sports is another billion dollar industry. Ice hockey is Canada's national sport. It also serves as an important symbol of national identity. ✓

Review Questions

1. How do Canada and the United States differ in their views of immigration?

_____

_____

_____

2. In what ways do French Canadians try to preserve their cultural heritage?

_____

_____

_____

✓ Reading Check

Which industries bring billions of dollars into the Canadian economy?

_____

_____

_____

CHAPTER
10

Section 1
Ontario and Quebec: Bridging Two Cultures

Objectives

1. Read about the seat of the Canadian government in Ontario.
2. Learn about the French cultural influence in Quebec.

Target Reading Skill

Use Context Clues What can you do when you see a word used in an unfamiliar way? Of course, you could look the word up in a dictionary. But often you can get a good idea of what the word means from the words around it.

Textbooks often tell you the meaning of new or unfamiliar words. In the sentences below, context clues help you find the meaning of *Canadian Shield*.

> The <u>northern region</u> is part of the Canadian Shield. Few people live in this <u>rocky land</u> with <u>harsh winters</u>.

The context clues have been underlined for you. What do they tell you about the Canadian Shield?

Vocabulary Strategy

Using Word Origins Many words in English come from ancient Greek or Latin words. In fact, once you know the meaning of Greek or Latin roots, you will be able to figure out the meaning of many English words, even if you have never seen the word before! For example, *phone* is a Greek root that means "sound or speech." So a microphone or telephone are things that you speak into. What is a "headphone"? Something that sends sound into your head!

Try this example: *Franco* means French. If you add the root *phone*, you have *Francophone*. Can you figure out what *Francophone* means? If you guessed "French-speaking," you are right!

Ontario

Ontario is one of the Canadian provinces. It lies between Hudson Bay and the Great Lakes. The northern region is part of the Canadian Shield. Few people live in this rocky land with harsh winters. The southern lowlands have milder winters and warm summers. About a third of Canada's entire population lives there.

Canada is a federation of 10 provinces and 3 territories. Each province has its own government. Just as in the United States, there is a federal or central government. Canada's central government is located in Ottawa, Ontario. The head of state is the British king or queen. This person is represented in Canada by the governor general. Canada's prime minister, however, leads the government. ✔

In the 1800s, Ontario was known as Upper Canada and Quebec was known as Lower Canada. Together, they formed the Province of Canada. Ottawa was chosen as the capital because it was located on the border of the two territories. As Canada added more provinces and territories, the capital stayed at Ottawa.

Each of Canada's provinces has a capital. Toronto is the capital of Ontario. Toronto is Canada's largest city. It is also the commercial and financial center of Canada. Located on Lake Ontario, it became a major trade and transportation center. After World War II, many European immigrants came to Toronto. Recently, immigrants have come from Asia. Nearly half the people who live in Toronto were born in other countries.

French Culture in Quebec

French culture in Quebec has its roots in the past. France claimed Quebec in the 1500s. For many years, the French and British fought for the region. In 1759, the British captured the city of Quebec. Within four years, France surrendered all its colonies east of the Mississippi River to the British.

> **Key Term**
>
> **federation** (fed ur AY shun) *n.* a union of states, groups, provinces, or nations

Even though the British won, tens of thousands of French colonists stayed in the region. Their descendants make up most of Quebec's population today. In Quebec's largest city, Montreal, and the surrounding areas, more than 65 percent of the population are Francophones.

In the 1960s, many Francophones became concerned about their language and culture. English was spoken at schools and at work. Most Francophones got jobs with lower pay. In 1960, the Liberal party, which supported Francophones, came to power in Quebec. Reforms were made in employment, education, and health care. This change became known as the Quiet Revolution.

However, the separatist movement still grew. In the 1970s, French became the official language of Quebec. Still, not everyone in Quebec wanted to separate from Canada. <u>In 1980, there was a referendum. In a referendum, people vote for or against an issue.</u> The people of Quebec voted against separation. In 1995, another vote was taken. This time, even more people voted for separation, but there was still not a majority. Separatists continue to work for independence. ✓

The people of Quebec take pride in their French culture. They celebrate it in many ways.

Review Questions

1. Who is the head of state in Canada?

_____

_____

2. What has the Canadian government done to support Francophones?

_____

_____

Key Terms

Francophone (FRANG koh fohn) *n.* a person who speaks French as his or her first language

Quiet Revolution (KWY ut rev uh LOO shun) *n.* a peaceful change in the government of Quebec

separatist (SEP ur uh tist) *n.* a person who wants Quebec to become an independent country

⊙ Target Reading Skill

Find the word *referendum* in the underlined sentences. If you do not know what a referendum is, look for a context clue. Here, the sentence following *referendum* is a definition of the term. What is a referendum?

_____

_____

_____

✓ Reading Check

What is the official language of Quebec?

_____

_____

Prepare to Read

Section 2
The Prairie Provinces: Canada's Breadbasket

Objectives

1. Learn why many immigrants came to the Prairie Provinces in the 1800s.
2. Read about how Canadians celebrate their cultural traditions.

Target Reading Skill

Interpret Nonliteral Meanings If you wanted to describe someone's height using literal language, you might say, "He is six feet, four inches tall." But if you used nonliteral language to say the same thing, you might say, "He is a giant." Nonliteral language uses vivid images to get ideas across.

This section is titled "The Prairie Provinces: Canada's Breadbasket." How can you tell that the section title uses nonliteral language? Ask yourself: "What does this language say about the Prairie Provinces?"

Vocabulary Strategy

Using Word Origins Words with French origins are common in Canada. This is because the French built early settlements there. There is an English word that describes the first people to settle in a place. The word is *pioneer*. It comes from a French word, *pionier*, that means "foot soldier." Foot soldiers often had to lead the way and do the hardest work, which describes what it is like to be a pioneer.

Try this example. The French word *voyager* means "to travel." A fur trader or trapper in Canada was called a *voyageur*. Can you see how the two words are related?

The Prairie Provinces

Manitoba, Saskatchewan, and Alberta are often called the Prairie Provinces. They are located on the largest prairie in the world. It stretches across the three provinces and into the central United States. Native peoples have lived there for thousands of years.

The way of life for native people was linked to the buffalo. Buffalo provided meat for food and hides for clothing. When people of European descent moved into the region, they quickly killed off most of the buffalo herds. At the same time, the government of Canada began to take over native peoples' land.

There began to be fewer native people. The Plains Indians did not have immunity to diseases brought by European immigrants. At the same time, the European population grew.

These settlers wanted to farm the prairie. The Canadian government encouraged immigration by offering free land to settlers. From 1900 to 1910, the population of Alberta alone increased by more than 500 percent.

Until the early 1900s, nearly all Canadians were native peoples or families from the early French and British settlers. Soon, immigrants from many different countries in Europe came to Canada. They farmed, mined, ranched, and hunted animals for fur.

Many of the European immigrants became wheat farmers. When the Canadian Pacific Railway was finished, settlers reached the Prairie Provinces more easily. It also allowed wheat to be carried more quickly to the rest of the world. <u>The wheat economy boomed.</u>

Today, more than three fourths of Canada's farmland is in the Prairie Provinces. Wheat is still the major crop. Saskatchewan produces more than half of Canada's wheat crop. Canada has become one the world's leading exporters of wheat. The region is known as Canada's Breadbasket. ✓

Key Terms

descent (dee SENT) *n.* a person's ancestry
immunity (ih MYOO nuh tee) *n.* a natural resistance to disease

---

Target Reading Skill

Read the underlined sentence to the left. What does *The wheat economy boomed* mean? *Hint:* The wheat economy of Canada did not literally make a booming noise!

_____

_____

_____

✓ Reading Check

Why is this region known as Canada's Breadbasket?

_____

_____

_____

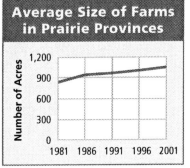

Number of Farms in Prairie Provinces	Average Size of Farms in Prairie Provinces

SOURCE: Statistics Canada   SOURCE: Statistics Canada

As you can see from the graphs, there were fewer farms in the Prairie Provinces in 2001 than in 1981. But farms in 2001 were larger than farms in 1981. This is because more and more of Canada's farms are corpo-
40 rate farms. But there are still more family-run farms in Canada than there are in the United States.

Celebrating Traditions

Each year, the cities of the Prairie Provinces celebrate their cultural heritage. The Calgary Stampede is a ten-day rodeo that honors the area's ranching legacy. It
45 offers events such as chuck-wagon races and bull riding. Klondike Days celebrate the gold rush. Events include a raft race and sourdough pancake breakfast. ☑

Each February, Festival du Voyageur is held in Winnipeg, Manitoba. It honors the French Canadian
50 fur-trading heritage. The Weyburn Wheat Festival pays tribute to the area's most important crop, wheat.

Review Questions

1. Which three provinces make up the Prairie Provinces?

_____

_____

_____

2. What attracted European immigrants to the Canadian Prairie Provinces?

_____

_____

_____

Prepare to Read

Section 3
British Columbia: Economic and Cultural Changes

Objectives

1. Find out about the people of the Canadian West.
2. Learn what the economy and culture of British Columbia are like.

Target Reading Skill

Use Context Clues Words work together to explain meaning. The meaning of a word may depend on its context. A word's context is the other words and sentences that surround it. The context gives you clues to the words meaning.

Try this example. Say that you do not know the meaning of the word *ethnic* in the following sentences:

The first people to live in British Columbia belonged to several <u>ethnic</u> groups and spoke many languages. Each group had its own customs.

You could ask yourself: "What information do the sentences give me about the word?" Answer: "I know that ethnic groups speak many languages and have their own customs. This tells me that an ethnic group must be people who share language and customs."

Vocabulary Strategy

Using Word Origins Often, you will read words that originally came from ancient Latin words. In this section, you will find the word *indigenous*. It comes from two Latin roots. The first one is *indus*. It means "in, or within." The second Latin root is *gignere*, which means "to be born." The word *indigenous* means "native" or someone "born within." The word is often used to describe the first people to inhabit an area.

The People of the Canadian West

1 The first people came to present-day British Columbia at least 10,000 years ago. They belonged to several ethnic groups and spoke many languages. Each group had its own customs. People along the coast caught
5 fish, whales, and shellfish. They also carved giant totem poles. Other groups lived and hunted in the inland forests.

In the late 1700s, European explorers arrived. The British built a fur-trading post on Vancouver (van KOO
10 vur) Island, off the coast of British Columbia. Fur traders introduced tools, European-style clothing, and ideas to the indigenous peoples. Then, in 1858, gold was discovered along the Fraser River.

A few years earlier, the British had founded a small town of traders and farmers called Victoria. One Sunday morning in 1858, an American paddlewheeler entered Victoria's harbor. The boat dropped off more than 400 men. They had come to mine gold in the area. Victoria's population doubled in one morning. Within weeks, tens of thousands more miners had arrived.

Two years later, gold was found in the Cariboo Mountains in eastern British Columbia. More miners came. Boomtowns sprang up almost overnight along the road. When the gold rush was over, many boom-
25 towns died out.

The new settlers were taking gold from the indigenous peoples' land. Native people had been the majority. But now they were the smallest minority of the population. They were pushed onto small reserves.
30 Laws banned many of their customs, religions, and languages. Children were taken from their parents and placed in government-run schools.

> **Key Terms**
>
> **totem pole** (TOHT um pohl) *n.* a tall, carved pole containing the symbols of a particular Native American group, clan, or family
> **boomtown** (boom town) *n.* a settlement that springs up quickly to serve the needs of miners

Today, the indigenous peoples of British Columbia take pride in their history and culture. Their art is thriving. But because of past injustice, they are demanding political rights and land. This has led to tension between indigenous peoples and other British Columbians.

In 1881, work began on the Canadian Pacific Railway. Its goal was to unite Canada. The railroad stretched all the way across Canada. Changes resulted from the railroad. Immigrants working on the railroad stayed after the railroad was done. Towns grew up along the railroad, and more newcomers moved in. ✅

Economics and Culture

The railroad connects all of Canada, but mountains form a barrier between British Columbia and the rest of Canada.

Trade links British Columbia with the Pacific Rim. The Pacific Rim countries include Japan, Australia, Chile, and Peru. They are the countries that border the Pacific Ocean. Another reason that people in British Columbia feel connected to the Pacific Rim is the varied population in British Columbia. More than 15 percent of the people are of Asian descent. ✅

British Columbia's television and film industry is another example of the province's link to other countries. British Columbia is the third-largest film production center in North America. Only Los Angeles and New York are bigger. More than 200 productions were filmed in the province in 2002. The film industry creates many jobs. Not all of them are for actors and directors. Businesses such as hotels, restaurants, and gas stations also benefit.

Review Questions

1. What brought people to British Columbia in the late 1800s?

_____

_____

2. Why does British Columbia have strong ties to the Pacific Rim?

_____

_____

✓ Reading Check

Why was the Canadian Pacific Railway built?

_____

_____

_____

✓ Reading Check

What is the Pacific Rim?

_____

_____

_____

Section 4
The Atlantic Provinces: Relying on the Sea

Objectives

1. Learn what life is like on the Atlantic coast.
2. Discover how maritime industries affect the provinces.

Target Reading Skill

Use Context Clues Context, or the words and sentences that surround a word, will help you understand a word you don't know. You can use cause and effect context clues to help you. They can show you how an unfamiliar word is related to either a cause or an effect. Clues to look for include: *because, since, then,* and *so.* Try to find the cause and effect clue in the example below.

> The Atlantic Provinces are often called the Maritime Provinces. That sums up the way of life there <u>because</u> much of the economy depends on fishing.

The cause and effect clue word is underlined. *Atlantic* and *fishing* are clues that tell you that *maritime* has to do with the sea.

Vocabulary Strategy

Using Word Origins Knowing the origin of a word part can help you figure out what the whole word means. For example, look at the word *aquaculture.* The word *aqua* is a Latin word that means "water."

Think of other words you know that begin with *aqua.* You probably know that an aquarium is a tank filled with water to keep fish. Perhaps you have gone to an aquatic center to swim. What do the words *aquatic* and *aquarium* have in common? Both have something to do with water.

Next, think of other words you know that end with *culture.* You know that agriculture refers to growing crops and raising livestock.

Now, put what you know together. *Aquaculture* means "growing things in water."

Section 4 Summary

Living on the Coast

1 Newfoundland and Labrador, Prince Edward Island, New Brunswick, and Nova Scotia are the Atlantic Provinces. They are located in eastern Canada on the Atlantic Ocean. Many of the people live on the coast.
5 The people of this region are mainly of English, Irish, Scottish, and French descent.

The Vikings were probably the first Europeans to build a colony here. Then in 1497, an English explorer named John Cabot called one of the islands *New Found*
10 *Land*. About 100 years later, it became England's first overseas colony. At first it was used mainly as a fishing station. In 2001, the province's name changed to Newfoundland and Labrador. You will learn that fishing has always been important in this area.

The province of Newfoundland and Labrador is the easternmost part of North America. It is closer to Ireland, across the Atlantic, than it is to New York State. Because of this, it is a transatlantic transportation and communications center. It is also close to the Grand Banks. The Grand Banks were once the best fishing grounds in the world.

Nova Scotia, New Brunswick, and Prince Edward Island were once part of Acadia. Acadia was a French settlement. France and England fought over the land
25 many times. Control went back and forth between the two countries. During the fighting, the Acadians did not take sides.

At one point, when the British were in control, they feared that the French Acadian settlers were loyal to
30 France. Therefore, they exiled the Acadians. Some settled in Quebec. Some moved to France or other French colonies. Others moved to present-day Louisiana. Their descendants there are known as Cajuns. ☑

Key Term

exile (EKS yl) *v.* to force someone to leave his or her native land or home

---

Target Reading Skill

Use the cause and effect context clue in the bracketed paragraph to discover what *transatlantic* means.

What is the cause and effect context clue?

_____

Cause: _____

Effect: _____

Transatlantic means: _____

_____

_____

✓ Reading Check

Why did the British exile the Acadians?

_____

_____

_____

Britain gained permanent control in 1763, at the end
of the Seven Years' War. Many Acadians then returned
to the area. But the British had taken over the farm-
lands. So the Acadians took up fishing and lumbering.

A Maritime Economy

The Atlantic Provinces are often called the Maritime
Provinces. That term sums up life there. Much of the
economy depends on fishing.

In the 1800s, there was great demand for fishing
boats. The shipbuilding industry grew. Through most
of the 1800s, this was Canada's leading shipbuilding
region. The forestry industry kept shipbuilders sup-
plied. Both industries helped the region's economy
grow. Many people still work at shipbuilding.

Fishing is another major industry. Until 1992, most
fishers caught cod. In that year, the government limited
how much cod fishers could catch. In 2003, it ended cod
fishing entirely. It took this action because the waters
had been overfished. Tens of thousands of fishing jobs
have been lost. Fishers are catching other types of fish
now. ✓

Aquaculture is a growing industry. Mussels are
grown on Canada's eastern coast. There are salmon
farms off the shores of New Brunswick.

Review Questions

1. Where are the Atlantic Provinces located?

_____

_____

_____

2. What industries did fishing help grow in the 1800s?

_____

_____

_____

Vocabulary Strategy

The word *maritime* comes from the
Latin root *mare*. This root means
"sea." Now that you know this,
explain why the Atlantic Provinces
are sometimes called the Maritime
Provinces.

_____

_____

_____

✓ Reading Check

Why did the government limit and
then end cod fishing?

_____

_____

_____

Prepare to Read

Section 5
The Northern Territories: New Frontiers

Objectives

1. Discover what life is like for people in Canada's far north.
2. Find out about the remote region of the Yukon Territory.
3. Understand how the new territory of Nunavut was formed.

Target Reading Skill

Use Context Clues Words and phrases often have different meanings in different situations. You may know a word, but the word does not make sense in the sentence.

For example, you could be watching a play when someone says that the *cast* was very talented. You would know that *cast* means the group of actors. But *cast* can also mean "to throw a fishing line" or "something you put on a broken arm."

What the word means in any situation depends on its context. Look for clues in the surrounding words, sentences, or paragraphs.

Vocabulary Strategy

Using Word Origins Many words that are used to describe government came from Latin. That is because countries all over the world were influenced by ancient Roman ideas about law and justice.

In this section you will study the Northern Territories. It may seem odd to learn about Latin word origins when reading about Canada's Northern Territories, but many of the words you will read in this section have Latin roots. They include *legislation, population, percent,* and *indigenous.*

Let's take a closer look at one word. The word *territory* comes from the Latin word *terra* which means "land." Usually if you see *terr* in an English word, it has something to do with land. For example, a *terrace* is a ledge cut into a hillside. And here is a fun one. A *terrier* is a little dog that likes to dig in the ground for small animals.

The aurora borealis gets its name from the Latin words for dawn and north. It is also known as the northern lights. This beautiful sight can be seen throughout northern Canada.

The Far North

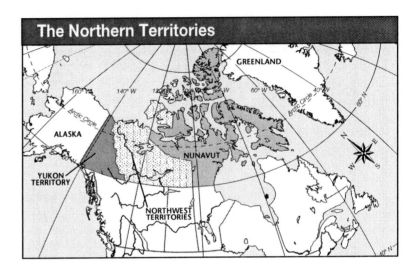

The Northern Territories

In addition to the provinces you learned about in the other sections, Canada has three territories. They are the Northwest Territories, Yukon Territory, and Nunavut (NOO nuh voot). The territories make up more than one third of Canada's land area. They stretch far north, into the Arctic Ocean. Less than one percent of Canada's population lives there. The main reason for this is the rugged terrain and harsh climate.

In the Northwest Territories, indigenous people make up almost half of the population. In Nunavut, Inuit people make up about 85 percent of the population. Only about 14 percent of the population of the Yukon is made up of native people. The rest of the population is of European or other ancestry.

Contact with Europeans and technology have both changed the way indigenous peoples live. For example, Inuit hunters today use snowmobiles instead of dogsleds to cross the frozen land.

Key Term

aurora borealis (aw RAWR uh bawr ee AL us) *n.* the colorful bands of light that can be seen in the skies of the Northern Hemisphere

The government of the Northern Territories differs
from the rest of Canada. Each territory has its own
legislature, similar to those of the provinces. However,
the federal government has a little more control over
the territories. Territories control local concerns, such as
education. But the federal government controls other
areas such as natural resources.

Forming New Territories

All of Canada's northern land used to be one big
territory called the Northwest Territories. Over time, it
was split into three separate territories.

Many people have heard about the Klondike Gold
Rush in the Yukon Territory. In 1896, gold was discovered in a branch of the Klondike River. Thousands of
miners swarmed in. In 1898, an act of Parliament made
the Yukon a separate territory. By the end of 1898, the
rush began to slow. The population dropped quickly.

Nunavut became the third Canadian territory in
1999. This fulfilled the Inuit people's dream of
governing themselves. The word *Nunavut* means
"our land" in Inuktitut. ✓

A new capital, Iqaluit (ee KAH loo eet), was built. The
construction provided many jobs. But Nunavut faces
challenges. Leaders must work to keep its economy
strong. The area now has Internet service, television,
and cellular phone service. Such modernization may be
a step in the right direction.

Review Questions

1. Why do so few people live in Canada's territories?

_____

_____

_____

2. What is the newest territory in Canada?

_____

_____

> **Key Term**
> **Inuktitut** (ih NOOK tih toot) *n.* the native language of the Inuit

Target Reading Skill

The word *branch* has several
meanings. You know that *branch*
often refers to a tree limb. It can
also mean something that goes off
from the main part. How is it used
in the bracketed paragraph?

_____

_____

_____

✓ Reading Check

Present-day Nunavut was once a
part of which territory?

_____

_____

_____

1. Many French Canadians want _____ to become a separate country.
   A. Ottawa
   B. Toronto
   C. Quebec
   D. Montreal

2. The Prairie Provinces are located
   A. in the Great Lakes.
   B. in the Northern Territories.
   C. on the largest prairie in the world.
   D. in British Columbia.

3. Because of its location, British Columbia is
   A. closer to Ireland than to New York.
   B. linked to the Pacific Rim.
   C. more British than Canadian.
   D. the only province that did not experience a gold rush.

4. The economy of the Atlantic Provinces depends upon
   A. oil.
   B. wheat.
   C. the sea.
   D. arts and crafts.

5. The Northern Territories have
   A. a mild climate.
   B. a large population of indigenous people.
   C. control over their own resources.
   D. no access to technology.

Short Answer Question

In what ways was the buffalo important to indigenous peoples in the Prairie Provinces?

_____

_____

_____

_____

Latin America

1. Learn where Latin America is located.
2. Discover the important landforms of Latin America.
3. Find out how Latin America's waterways have affected the region.

Preview and Set a Purpose Reading a textbook is different from reading a novel or the newspaper. There is a special way to read a textbook. To make your reading powerful, preview and set a purpose for your reading.

Before you read the next two pages, take a minute to preview them. Look at the title above, "Land and Water," and then the three objectives. Now flip through the next two pages and read the headings and the map. These parts tell you what to expect to learn from this section. As you preview, you set your purpose for reading. Your purpose is to find details that give more meaning to the title, objectives, headings, and map.

The objectives, headings, and map all relate to "Land and Water." As you keep reading, you can expect to learn about Latin America's location, and what its land and water are like.

Using Context Clues to Determine Meaning A word's **context** is the other words, phrases, and sentences that surround it. Think of context as clues to a word's meaning. Words work together to communicate meaning. The meaning of a word may depend on its context.

Try this example. Suppose that you did not know the meaning of the word *tributaries* in this sentence:

"The Amazon River gathers power from many tributaries." You could ask yourself: "What information does the sentence give me about the word?" Answer: "It tells me that tributaries are the source of power." Then ask: "What things can provide power?" Answer: "Perhaps many streams feeding into the river would increase its power."

Tributaries are smaller streams and rivers that flow into the larger river and give it power.

Section 1 Summary

1 Latin America is a region of **variety** and **contrast**.

Where Is Latin America?

Latin America is in the Western Hemisphere, south of the United States. Latin America is divided into three smaller regions. They are (1) Middle America; (2) the
5 Caribbean (ka ruh BEE un); and (3) South America. South America is a continent. ✓

Landforms of Latin America

Middle America is made of mountains. They are on
10 both sides of Mexico's central plateau. Along the east and west coasts of Mexico
15 are narrow plains. Central America is an isthmus. It joins North and South
20 America. With so many mountains, Middle America has a lot of active volcanoes. Ash from the volcanoes makes the soil fertile.

   The Caribbean is a region of islands. Some of the
25 smaller islands are made of the skeletons of tiny sea animals. These skeletons make up a rocklike material called coral. The larger islands are the tops of volcanoes that are mostly under water. A few of these volcanoes are still active.

Regions of Latin America

CARIBBEAN ISLANDS

MEXICO AND CENTRAL AMERICA

ATLANTIC OCEAN

PACIFIC OCEAN

SOUTH AMERICA

N
W — E
S

Mexico and Central America
Caribbean Islands
South America

© Pearson Education, Inc., Publishing as Pearson Prentice Hall. All rights reserved.

Target Reading Skill

What is your purpose in reading this paragraph?

_____

_____

Underline the words or phrases in the paragraph that answer the question in the heading. Did you meet your purpose in reading this part? Why or why not?

_____

_____

_____

✓ Reading Check

What three regions make up Latin America?

1. _____

2. _____

3. _____

Key Terms

Middle America (MID ul uh MEHR ih kuh) *n.* Mexico and Central America

plateau (pla TOH) *n.* a large, level area that is higher than the land around it

isthmus (IS mus) *n.* a strip of land that has water on both sides and joins two larger pieces of land

Vocabulary Strategy

What do the words *natural highways* mean in the underlined sentence? Underline the words you find in the surrounding words, phrases, or sentences that provide clues to the meaning of the words.

What do the words mean?

_____

_____

✓ **Reading Check**

Circle the names of the three rivers that form the Río de la Plata system.

30   South America has many different landforms. Perhaps the most impressive is the huge Andes Mountains. The Andes run 5,500 miles (8,900 kilometers) along the western coast. Although the Andes are steep, the rich soil supports farming. South America 35 also has rolling plains called highlands. To the south are the pampas. The Amazon Basin contains the largest tropical rain forest in the world. ✓

Latin America's Waterways

Latin America has some of the longest and largest bodies of water in the world. These waterways are impor- 40 tant to the people of the region. <u>Rivers act as natural highways in places where it is hard to build roads</u>. Rivers also provide food and power for electricity.

   Latin America's Amazon River is the second-longest river in the world. The Amazon flows 4,000 45 miles (6,437 kilometers) from Peru across Brazil into the Atlantic Ocean. It carries more water than any other river in the world. The Amazon gathers power from more than 1,000 tributaries.

   Latin America has many other useful waterways. 50 The Paraná, Paraguay, and Uruguay rivers make up the Río de la Plata system. It separates Argentina and Uruguay. In Venezuela, people use the Orinoco River and Lake Maracaibo (mar uh KY boh). ✓

Review Questions

1. What kinds of landforms exist in Latin America?

_____

_____

2. Why are waterways important to Latin America?

_____

_____

Key Terms

pampas (PAM puz) *n.* flat grasslands in South America
rain forest (rayn FAWR ist) *n.* a thick evergreen forest that gets a lot of rain
Amazon River (AM uh zahn RIV uhr) *n.* a long river in northern South America
tributary (TRIB yoo tehr ee) *n.* a river or stream that flows into a larger river

---

CHAPTER 11

Objectives

1. Find out what kinds of climate Latin America has.
2. Learn what factors influence climate in Latin America.
3. Understand how climate and vegetation influence the ways people live.

Target Reading Skill

Preview and Predict Before you read, make a prediction or a guess about what you will be learning. Predicting is another way to set a purpose for reading. It will help you remember what you read. Follow these steps: (1) Preview the section title, objectives, headings, and table on the pages in Section 2. (2) Predict something you might learn about Latin America. Based on your preview, you will probably predict that you will learn more about Latin America's climate and plants.

List two facts that you predict you will learn about Latin America's climate and plants.

_____

_____

As you read, check your predictions. How correct were they? If they were not very accurate, try to pay closer attention when you preview.

Vocabulary Strategy

Using Context Clues to Determine Meaning You will probably come across words you haven't seen before when you read. Sometimes you can pick up clues about the meaning of an unfamiliar word by reading the words, phrases, and sentences that surround it. The underlined words in the sentences below give clues to the meaning of the word *dense*.

The Amazon rain forest is *dense* with plants and trees. The plant life is so crowded that almost no sunlight reaches the ground.

Unfamiliar Word	Clues	Meaning
dense	so crowded no sunlight	thick, close together crowded

[1] Every few years, strange weather strikes Latin America. Areas that are usually dry get heavy rains instead. Wet places are hit by drought. El Niño is to blame. El Niño is a warming of the ocean water along [5] the western coast of South America. This warming changes the weather around the world. El Niño is one of many things that affect climate in Latin America.

The Climates of Latin America

The climate in Latin America varies a lot from region to region. The temperature can be below freezing in the [10] Andes Mountains. In the Amazon Basin, it may reach 90°F (32°C). Some areas of the Amazon Basin get 80 inches (203 centimeters) of rain each year! Latin America also has some of the driest places on Earth. Caribbean climate is usually sunny and warm. But [15] from June to November the region is often hit with fierce storms called hurricanes.

Many parts of Latin America have a tropical wet climate. That means they have hot, humid, rainy weather almost every day. Other parts of Latin America have a [20] tropical wet and dry climate. These areas are just as hot, but the rainy season is shorter. Parts of Mexico and Brazil and most of the Caribbean have a tropical wet and dry climate. ✔

Much of Argentina, Uruguay, and Paraguay has a [25] humid subtropical climate. Summers are hot and rainy, with cool, damp winters. Farther south is Patagonia (pat uh GOH nee uh) where the climate is dry.

What Factors Affect Climate?

Three key factors affect climate in Latin America. One factor is elevation. Location and wind patterns are the [30] other two key factors. The table at the top of the next page shows the effects of all three factors.

Target Reading Skill

Based on what you have read so far, are you on target with your predictions? Explain why or why not.

_____

_____

_____

✓ Reading Check

Describe a tropical wet and dry climate.

_____

_____

_____

Key Terms

El Niño (el NEEN yoh) *n.* a warming of the ocean water along the western coast of South America

elevation (el uh VAY shun) *n.* the height of the land above sea level

Causes	Effects
Elevation	The higher the elevation, the colder the temperature
Location	Regions close to the Equator are warmer than those farther away ✓
Wind patterns	Sea breezes keep temperatures mild and bring more rain

Climate, Plants, and People

The Amazon rain forest is dense with thousands of types of plants. The air is hot and moist. In contrast, the Atacama (ah tah KAH mah) Desert in Chile has few
35 signs of life because it is very dry. Latin America's physical features make such climate extremes possible.

Many regions of Latin America have less extreme climates. They have different kinds of vegetation, or plant life. Temperature and rainfall affect what plants
40 grow in a region. They also affect what crops people can grow. For example, sugar cane, coffee, and bananas need warm weather and much rain. These three crops are important in Latin America. The economy of many countries depends on exporting these crops.
45 Elevation also affects vegetation. The higher the elevation, the cooler and drier it is. Plants must be able to survive in these conditions. ✓

Review Questions

1. What are four climates common in Latin America?

_____

_____

2. How does climate affect the people and the economy of Latin America?

_____

_____

Key Term

economy (ih KAHN uh mee) *n.* the ways that goods and services are made and brought to people

Vocabulary Strategy

Look at the word *vegetation* in the underlined sentence. Underline the surrounding words or phrases that are clues to the word's meaning.

✓ Reading Check

Describe how elevation affects the vegetation of a region.

_____

_____

_____

Objectives

1. Learn which natural resources are important to Latin America.
2. Discover why a one-resource economy can be dangerous for Latin American nations.

Target Reading Skill

Preview and Ask Questions Before you read Section 3, preview the titles, objectives, headings, and illustrations to see what you will read about. What do you think are the most important concepts in the section?

Now write two questions that will help you understand or remember these important concepts or facts. For example, you might ask, "What are the resources of Latin America?"

As you read, keep asking questions about what you think will come next. Then check to see if what you read answers your questions. Were you close with your predictions?

Vocabulary Strategy

Using Context Clues to Determine Meaning It is common for some English words to have more than one meaning. Remember context clues? Use them to figure out a word's meaning. The word *back*, for example, in the sentences below, is used in two different ways.

He wrote his answers on the **back** of the worksheet.

By using context clues, you can figure out that in this sentence, *back* means "reverse side."

She asked her friends to **back** her plan.

By using context clues, you can figure out that in this sentence, *back* means "support."

Latin America's Resources

1 Latin America's natural resources are as varied as its climate. The region is rich in oil and natural gas. <u>There are deposits of many minerals underneath the land of Latin America</u>. Forest areas spread across both Mexico
5 and South America. In Mexico, trees are used for lumber and paper products. In South America, trees provide wood for building and coconuts for eating. Important medicines come from rain forest plants. ✓

The rich soil and good climate in Latin American
10 countries are perfect for farming. The people there grow coffee, sugar cane, bananas, cotton, beans called cacao (kuh KAY oh) to make chocolate, and other crops. On the coast, people harvest fish in the region's waters.

Huge dams in Central America use the power of
15 water to produce hydroelectricity.

Resources and the Economy

Not every Latin American country has the same amount of natural resources. Some countries have many, but some countries have very few. Some countries do not have the money to develop the resources
20 they do have.

Sometimes a country's economy depends too much on one resource or one crop. This is called a one-resource economy. This type of economy can cause problems. For example, there can be a drop in the price
25 people will pay for the resource. Or bad weather could destroy a country's one main crop. When such problems happen, it hurts the country's whole economy.

Vocabulary Strategy

What is the meaning of the word *deposit* in the underlined sentence? (Hint: It does not mean "to put money in the bank.")

_____

_____

_____

✓ **Reading Check**

Circle the names of products made from South America's forests.

Key Terms

natural resources (NACH ur al REE sawrs uz) *n.* things found in nature that people can use to meet their needs

hydroelectricity (hy droh ee lek TRIS ih tee) *n.* electricity made by fast-moving water

one-resource economy (wun REE sawrs ih KAHN uh mee) *n.* an economy based mainly on one resource or one crop

What questions could you ask about the chart, based on the heading? Does the chart answer your questions? Were you able to predict what would be covered in it?

_____

_____

_____

_____

The chart below shows the cycle of problems that can occur when a country's economy depends too much on
30 one resource.

Problems of a One-Resource Economy

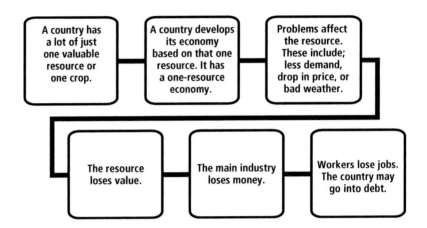

A country has a lot of just one valuable resource or one crop. → A country develops its economy based on that one resource. It has a one-resource economy. → Problems affect the resource. These include; less demand, drop in price, or bad weather. → The resource loses value. → The main industry loses money. → Workers lose jobs. The country may go into debt.

✓ Reading Check

Circle the items Brazil is now developing to help diversify its economy.

The countries of Latin America are trying to diversify their economies. Many of them are building new industries. They are planting a wider variety of crops. For example, Brazil has been building its industries.
35 That way, it does not have to depend so much on agriculture. Brazil now exports machinery, steel, and chemicals. The governments of Latin America are looking for ways to avoid the dangers of a one-resource economy. ✓

Review Questions

1. What are some of Latin America's natural resources?

_____

_____

_____

2. Why is a one-resource economy dangerous to Latin American nations?

_____

_____

_____

> **Key Term**
> **diversify** (duh VUR suh fy) v. to add different types of things

1. The three geographic regions of Latin America are
   A. Mexico, Brazil, and Peru.
   B. the Amazon, the Andes, and the Río de la Plata system.
   C. Middle America, the Caribbean, and South America.
   D. coral, isthmus, and tributary.

2. The Amazon River is
   A. Mexico's greatest resource.
   B. the cause of hurricanes in the Caribbean each year.
   C. next to the Andes Mountains in Chile.
   D. one of the largest rivers in the world.

3. A humid subtropical climate is
   A. one in which the weather is hot and rainy all year round.
   B. hot, but the rainy season lasts only part of the year.
   C. similar to the climate in parts of the southern United States.
   D. found in the area called Patagonia.

4. Climate in Latin America is influenced by nearness to the Equator,
   A. vegetation, and the economy.
   B. elevation, and wind patterns.
   C. location, and wind speed.
   D. rivers, and deserts.

5. The amount of natural resources in Latin America can best be
   described as
   A. the same throughout the region.
   B. similar to that of the United States.
   C. a sign of the region's economic diversity.
   D. uneven from country to country.

Short Answer Question

How does the physical geography of Latin America affect the people
who live there?

_____

_____

_____

_____

_____

Section 1 Early Civilizations of Middle America

1. Find out what Mayan civilization was like.
2. Learn about the Aztec empire and Aztec society.

 Target Reading Skill

Reread Rereading means to read something again. Sometimes you may not understand a sentence or a paragraph the first time you read it. When this happens, rereading can help. When you reread a sentence or paragraph, you may find clues that help you clear up your confusion. As you read, ask yourself questions. What are the subjects of the sentences? What action is taking place? Look for details. If the details don't lead you to the main idea, look for words or phrases that help you. Sometimes you will find key words that will provide clues to help you understand the information.

Try these steps:

1. Look for connections among the words and sentences.
2. Repeat the sentences slowly to yourself after you have read them once.
3. Add up facts that you do understand. Then see if you can find the main idea.

Vocabulary Strategy

Using Context to Clarify Meaning Many times when you are reading you will be stumped by a word you do not know. Sometimes when you come across new words in your text, they are often defined for you. Sometimes there is a brief definition in the same sentence. Often, the word *or* is used to introduce the definition. At other times, other words in the sentence may give you an idea of the word's meaning.

Look at the following examples from this section.

Mayas performed religious ceremonies that included <u>human sacrifice</u>. They *offered human life to please their gods.*

They forced the conquered people to pay <u>tribute</u>, or *taxes.*

As you can see, both of these examples provide definitions to clarify the meaning of unfamiliar words.

Section 1 Summary

The Mayas

1 The Mayas were an ancient people who lived in Central America and southern Mexico. Their civilization thrived from A.D. 300 to A.D. 900. The Mayas built great cities, such as Tikal (tee KAHL), in present-day
5 Guatemala, and Copán, in present-day Honduras.

Large temples often stood in the middle of Mayan cities. The cities served as economic, political, and religious centers. Different Mayan cities often fought one another in wars.

10 Mayan priests studied the stars and planets. They developed two calendars. One was used to decide when to hold religious celebrations. The other was used to follow the seasons.

The Mayas also came up with a system of writing called hieroglyphics. Hierogyphics used signs and symbols. With a writing system, Mayans were able to write books.

Farmers worked in fields near the cities. Their most important crop was maize, or corn. They also grew beans, squash, peppers, avocados, and papayas.

In about A.D. 900, Mayan cities began to decline. Nobody knows why. It may have been because war, disease, drought, or starvation killed many of their people. Or the people may have rebelled against the
25 control of the priests and nobles. Still, Mayas stayed in the area. Today, millions of Mayas live in Mexico and northern Central America. ✓

The Aztec Empire

30 In the 1400s, another great civilization arose in Middle America. It was created by the Aztecs. They arrived in the area in the 1100s. In 1325, the Aztecs settled on an

Vocabulary Strategy

The key terms *hieroglyphics* and *maize* are in the bracketed paragraphs. Underline the words in the sentences that tell you the definitions of the key terms.

✓ Reading Check

What are some possible reasons the Mayan cities began to decline?

_____

_____

Key Terms

hieroglyphics (hy ur oh GLIF iks) *n.* a system of writing that uses pictures or symbols instead of an alphabet
maize (mayz) *n.* corn

Do you remember the location of Tenochtitlán? Go back and reread. Look for each reference to it. Underline the word Tenochtitlán each time it appears in the summary.

island in Lake Texcoco. They changed the swampy lake into a great city called Tenochtitlán. From there the Aztecs ruled their empire.

The Aztecs began conquering other people. They forced the conquered to pay tribute, or taxes, which made the Aztecs rich. An emperor ruled over Aztec lands. Nobles and priests helped him. Soldiers fought wars to add land to the empire. Most of the people in the empire were farmers who grew corn, squash, and beans. They used irrigation to water their crops. They created new farmland by building floating gardens.

Tenochtitlán was a fantastic city. It had huge temples, busy markets, wide streets and canals, floating gardens, and a zoo. The emperor and nobles lived in beautiful palaces. They had many slaves to serve them. Priests performed ceremonies such as human sacrifice to please their gods. Priests used a calendar based on the Maya calendar. Like the Mayas, the Aztecs kept records using hieroglyphics.

Aztec doctors made medicines from plants. They also set broken bones and practiced dentistry.

A strong army protected trade routes. Traders could travel long distances in safety. Because the Aztecs did not have pack animals to carry loads, they used people called porters. Trade was usually done by barter. To barter is to trade goods for other goods, instead of paying for them with money. ✓

Unlike the Mayas, the Aztecs did not abandon their cities. Instead, people from far away conquered them.

Review Questions

1. What happened to the Mayas in about A.D. 900?

_____

_____

_____

2. Briefly describe Tenochtitlán.

_____

_____

_____

Reading Check

How was trade carried out in the Aztec empire?

_____

_____

Key Term

Tenochtitlán (teh nawch tee TLAHN) *n.* the capital city of the Aztec empire, located where Mexico City now stands

Objectives

1. Find out how the Incas created their empire.
2. Understand what Incan civilization was like.
3. Learn about the life of Incas today.

Target Reading Skill

Read Ahead When you read and come across a word or an idea you are not sure of—keep reading! The word or idea may be explained later on. Sometimes a word is defined after it has been used, or the main idea of one paragraph may have more details to support it in later paragraphs.

In the first sentence on the next page, after the heading The Rise of the Incas, you may not understand what Cuzco is. By reading ahead, you will find out that it was a village in the Andes Mountains that became the Incan capital.

Vocabulary Strategy

Using Context to Clarify Meaning Textbooks often use unfamiliar words. To figure out the meaning of a word, look for clues in the context. Context refers to the words, sentences, and paragraphs just before and after the word. As you read this section, use this graphic organizer as a guide.

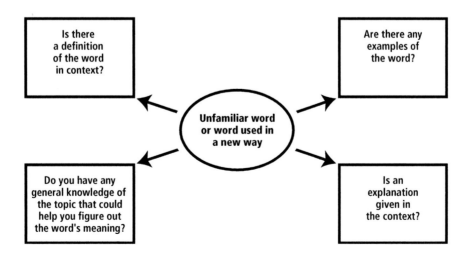

Vocabulary Strategy

Look for at least one word in this section that is new to you. Use the graphic organizer to help you figure out what the word means from the context. Write it below, followed by a brief definition. (Use a word other than *quipu*.)

_____

_____

_____

✓ Reading Check

What did Pachacuti do to people who were disloyal?

_____

_____

Target Reading Skill

What does the word *quipu* mean? Read ahead to see if it is defined for you. Underline the definition.

The Rise of the Incas

¹ The Incas first settled in Cuzco in about A.D. 1200. Cuzco, a city in present-day Peru, was a village in the Andes Mountains. It became the Incan capital. Most Incas were farmers who grew maize and other crops.

⁵   In 1438, Pachacuti (pahch ah KOO tee) became ruler of the Incas. He conquered the people of the Andes and the Pacific coast. His empire ran from Lake Titicaca north to the city of Quito. Pachacuti forced people who were not loyal off their land. ✓

¹⁰   Pachacuti's son, Topa Inca, later became emperor. He expanded the Incan empire to include land in present-day Ecuador, Peru, Bolivia, Chile, and Argentina.

Incan Civilization

The Incan emperor carefully chose nobles to govern each province. Nobles conducted a census so that the ¹⁵people could be taxed. The government cared for poor, sick, or elderly Incas.

    Without a written language, Incan officials and traders relied on a quipu to keep track of information. Every quipu had a main cord with several colored ²⁰strings attached to it. Each color stood for a different item. Knots of different sizes stood for numbers.

    The Incas needed a fast and safe way to travel through the rugged Andes Mountains. They built a large road system. This helped the government rule the ²⁵empire. Relay runners used the roads to carry messages from one place to another. Incan armies and traders used the roads for speedy travel. Experts built rope bridges to cross the deep valleys or gorges.

    Incas also built canals and aqueducts to irrigate ³⁰land that would otherwise be too dry to grow crops.

Key Terms

Cuzco (KOOS koh) *n.* capital of the Incan empire

Topa Inca (TOH puh ING kuh) *n.* Inca emperor who expanded their empire

census (SEN suhs) *n.* an official count of all the people who live in an area

quipu (KEE poo) *n.* knotted strings used by the Incas to track information

aqueduct (AHK wuh dukt) *n.* a pipe or channel that carries water from a distant source

Incan engineers were very skilled at building with stone. They built cities, palaces, temples, and fortresses without the use of modern tools. They used only hammers and chisels to cut stones so perfectly that they fit together without mortar or cement. Some of these buildings can still be seen in Peru. Even today, the stones fit together so tightly that a piece of paper cannot be slipped between them. The most famous Incan ruin is called Machu Picchu (MAH choo PEEK choo). The ruin shows buildings, stairs carved into the side of the mountain, and roads cut into rock. ✓

Like the Mayas and the Aztecs, Incas worshipped many gods and practiced human sacrifice. One of their most important gods was the sun god, Inti. The Incas believed that Inti was their parent. They called themselves the "children of the sun." Another important god was Viracocha (vee ruh KOH chuh), the creator of all the people of the Andes.

The Quechua: Descendants of the Incas

The Spanish conquered the Incan empire in the 1500s. However, people descended from the Incas still live in Peru, Ecuador, Bolivia, Chile, and Colombia. They speak Quechua (KECH wuh), the Incan language. Many of the Quechua live high in the Andes. They are cut off from many parts of modern life, but they are still affected by it. Most of the Quechua live by farming, using methods similar to those of the Incas. They also spin wool and weave fabric much as the Incas did. Their fabrics and clothing styles also reflect their Incan heritage. ✓

Review Questions

1. Where and when did the Incas create their empire?

_____

_____

_____

2. Why were good roads and bridges important to the Incas?

_____

_____

_____

Objectives

1. Learn why Europeans sailed to the Americas.
2. Find out how conquistadors conquered the Aztecs and the Incas.
3. Understand how the Spanish empire was organized and how colonization affected the Americas.

 **Target Reading Skill**

Paraphrase When you paraphrase, you reword what you have read in your own words. Use paraphrasing to rewrite sentences that are long or wordy, or ideas that are hard to understand.

Look at this example: "Settlers from Spain, Portugal, and other European nations began arriving in what came to be called Latin America." You could paraphrase this by saying: "Settlers from Europe came to what is now Latin America."

Vocabulary Strategy

Using Context to Clarify Meaning. Look for context clues to help you figure out the meaning of words you do not know. Are there other words in the sentence, paragraph, or section title that can help you?

This chart shows how the subject of the section and word clues can help you figure out word meaning.

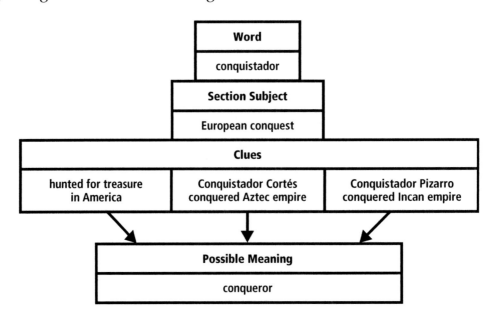

Section 3 Summary

Europeans Arrive in the Americas

1 In the 1400s, Spain and Portugal were both looking for new trade routes to Asia. The Italian explorer Christopher Columbus thought he could get to Asia by sailing west across the Atlantic Ocean. Queen
5 Isabella of Spain paid for his trip. Columbus spotted land on October 12, 1492. He thought he had reached the East Indies in Asia. Because of that, Columbus called the people he met Indians.

Spain and Portugal competed for land in the
10 Americas. Then, in 1494, they signed the Treaty of Tordesillas (tor day SEE yas). It created an imaginary line from the North Pole to the South Pole. Spain got the right to settle and trade west of the line. Portugal could settle and trade east of the line. ✓

The Success of the Conquistadors

15 Spanish rulers allowed the conquistadors to hunt for treasure and settle in America. Conquistadors agreed to give Spain part of any treasures they found.

The conquistador Hernán Cortés went to Mexico in 1519. The Aztecs' enemies helped Cortés attack
20 Tenochtitlán and kill the Aztec emperor, Moctezuma. The Aztecs surrendered in 1521, and Spain claimed the region.

Another Spanish conquistador, Francisco Pizarro, arrived in South America in 1531. He had 180 soldiers.
25 By 1535, Pizarro conquered most of the Incan empire.

In only 15 years, the Spanish had defeated the two greatest empires in the Americas. The Spanish were able to do this because they had better weapons, including guns and cannons. They also brought new
30 diseases that wiped out whole villages. ✓

Key Terms

Christopher Columbus (KRIS tuh fur kuh LUM bus) *n.* Italian explorer sailing for Spain who landed in the West Indies in 1492
conquistador (kahn KEES tuh dawr) *n.* a conqueror who claimed and ruled land in the Americas for Spain in the 1500s
Hernán Cortés (her NAHN kohr TEZ) *n.* conquistador who conquered the Aztecs
Moctezuma (mahk tih ZOO muh) *n.* ruler of the Aztecs
Francisco Pizarro (frahn SEES koh pea SAHR oh) *n.* conquistador who conquered the Incas

---

✓ Reading Check

Why did Spain and Portugal become rivals?

_____

_____

✓ Reading Check

What are two reasons the conquistadors were able to conquer the Aztecs and the Incas?

1. _____

_____

2. _____

_____

Colonization

Settlers from Europe began arriving in Latin America. The Catholic Church sent missionaries to spread Christianity to Native Americans. Some settlers came to farm or to look for gold or other riches.

Spain ruled most of the Americas south of what is now the United States. The territory was divided into provinces. The king chose viceroys to rule for him. The newcomers used force to control their colonies.

The two most important provinces were New Spain
40 and Peru. The people with the most power came from Spain or had Spanish parents. People of mixed Spanish and Native American ancestry were called mestizos. Native Americans had the least power.

Spain gave its settlers encomiendas (en koh MYEN
45 dahs). These were rights to demand taxes or work from Native Americans. At first, Native Americans were forced to work only on haciendas. When silver was found, they also had to work in the mines.

Many Native Americans died from overwork, lack
50 of food, and illness. As their population dropped, the Spanish imported African slaves to do the work. ✓

In Brazil, a colony of Portugal, most settlers lived near the coast. They also relied on the forced labor of Native Americans and African slaves.

Review Questions

1. What agreement did the Spanish rulers make with the conquistadors?

_____

_____

_____

2. How was Spain's empire governed?

_____

_____

_____

Key Terms

mestizo (meh STEE zoh) *n.* in Latin America, a person of mixed Spanish and Native American ancestry
hacienda (hah see EN dah) *n.* a large farm or plantation

Read the bracketed paragraph carefully, and then paraphrase it, or restate it in your own words.

_____

_____

_____

_____

Vocabulary Strategy

From context clues, write a definition of the word *province*, which is underlined twice above. Circle words or phrases in the text that helped you write your definition.

_____

_____

_____

✓ Reading Check

Why did the Native American population decline?

_____

_____

_____

Objectives

1. Learn what events inspired revolutions in Latin America.
2. Find out how Mexico gained its independence.
3. Discover how Bolívar and San Martín helped bring independence to South America.

Target Reading Skill

Summarize A good way to better understand what you read is to pause once in a while and summarize what you have read. To summarize, write a short statement of what you have read. Focus on the main points. Leave out the less important details. A summary is shorter than the original text. When you summarize, keep the main ideas or facts in the correct order. A good summary also makes connections between events or details.

Here's an example:

Simón Bolívar dreamed for years of uniting South America into one country, which would be a "United States of South America."

It could be summarized like this:

Simón Bolívar wanted to create a "United States of South America."

Vocabulary Strategy

Using Context to Clarify Meaning You don't always need a dictionary to figure out the meaning of a word. In this workbook, key terms appear in blue. They are defined in a box at the bottom of the page they appear on. Looking for the definition may interrupt your reading or cause you to lose your place. Try reading the passage from beginning to end to see if you can figure out what the word means from the context. Then look at the definition to see if you were right.

Try this example:

Criollos had Spanish parents, education, and wealth, but very little political power. That is because only people born in Spain could hold government office.

Circle the clues that help you figure out the meaning of *criollos*. Check the definition in the box on the next page to see if you were right.

The Seeds of Revolution

1 People in Latin American countries wanted freedom. They were inspired by two revolutions. In the 1770s and early 1780s British colonies in North America won freedom from British rule. In 1789, the people of France 5 rose up against their rulers. ✓

In Haiti, slaves rebelled against their masters. A former slave, Toussaint L'Ouverture, led the people in their fight for freedom. After more than 10 years of fighting, the people won. In 1804, Haiti became an 10 independent country.

Criollos in Latin America were especially interested in these events because they could not hold government office. Only people born in Spain could hold government offices. Criollos were often wealthy and well 15 educated. They liked the idea that people had the right to govern themselves. Yet, the slave revolt in Haiti frightened them. Criollos wanted independence from Spain, but they wanted power for themselves.

Independence in Mexico

The Mexican fight for independence from Spain began 20 in 1810. It was started by Miguel Hidalgo (mee GEL hee DAHL goh), a criollo priest. His call for revolution attracted some 80,000 fighters. Most of the fighters were mestizos or Native Americans. The government captured and killed Hidalgo in 1811. ✓

25 The struggle for freedom was taken over by Agustín de Iturbide (aw guh STEEN deh ee toor BEE day). Like Hidalgo, Iturbide was a criollo. But many wealthy people who had been afraid to join Hidalgo trusted Iturbide. With their support, Mexico won independ-30 ence in 1821.

✓ Reading Check

Which revolutions inspired ideas of independence in Latin America?

_____

_____

✓ Reading Check

What groups made up most of Hidalgo's army?

_____

_____

_____

Key Terms

revolution (rev uh LOO shun) *n.* overthrow of a government, with another taking its place
Toussaint L'Ouverture (too SAN loo vehr TOOR) *n.* leader of Haiti's fight for independence
criollo (kree OH yoh) *n.* a person with Spanish parents who was born in Latin America

South American Independence

Two important revolutionary leaders in South America were Simón Bolívar and José de San Martín. Bolívar freed a large area in South America known as Gran Colombia. It included the future countries of
35 Colombia, Venezuela, Ecuador, and Panama.

San Martín led the fight for freedom in Argentina, Chile, and Peru. He was a bold and popular leader. San Martín often surprised the Spanish, by attacking from the sea or the Andes.

40 By 1825, the Spanish had been driven out of South America. Spain ruled only Cuba and Puerto Rico.

Bolívar wanted to unite South America into a single country. Gran Colombia was the first step. But Latin America is a huge area. It is divided by the Andes and
45 dense rain forests. Other caudillos, or leaders, wanted little to do with Bolívar. Bolívar cared about the people he governed. Other caudillos wanted only power and riches. ✅

Portugal's colony, Brazil, became independent with-
50 out a fight. In the early 1800s the Portuguese royal family came to Brazil. When the king returned to Europe, he left his son Dom Pedro to rule Brazil. Dom Pedro did something that the king was not expecting. He declared Brazil independent in 1822.

Review Questions

1. Why did criollos want independence?

_____

_____

2. What were the achievements of Bolívar, San Martín, and Dom Pedro?

_____

_____

_____

> **Key Terms**
>
> **Simón Bolívar** (see MOHN boh LEE vahr) *n.* a South American revolutionary leader
> **José de San Martín** (hoh SAY deh sahn mahr TEEN) *n.* a South American revolutionary leader
> **caudillo** (kaw DEE yoh) *n.* a military officer who rules a country very strictly

---

Target Reading Skill

Read the bracketed paragraph and then write a summary of it.

You might use *How San Martín Defeated the Spanish* as a title for your summary.

_____

_____

_____

✓ Reading Check

What are two reasons that South America was not united into one country?

_____

_____

_____

_____

Objectives

1. Learn how Latin American caudillos and foreign involvement contributed to the region's troubled past.
2. Find out how Latin American nations are struggling to improve their economies and the welfare of their people.

Target Reading Skill

Reread or Read Ahead Both rereading and reading ahead can help you understand words and ideas in the text.

Read ahead to see if information in the text helps you to understand the word or ideas. A word may be defined after its first use or the main idea may be discussed later.

If you do not understand something in the sentence or paragraph, try going back and rereading it. Then look for details you may have missed.

Vocabulary Strategy

Using Context to Clarify Meaning Sometimes you read a word you recognize, but it does not seem to make sense in the sentence. Many words have more than one meaning. What a word means depends on its context. Look for clues in the surrounding words, sentences, or paragraphs. For example, the word *press* has many meanings. By using context, you can tell what meaning the author had in mind.

Some common definitions for *press* are listed in the chart below, along with examples in context.

Word	Definitions	Examples
press	to push against	Press the button.
	a machine used to apply pressure	It was stamped out in a metal press.
	printing equipment (short for printing press)	The newspaper has gone to press.
	newspapers, magazines, and journalists	Freedom of the press is guaranteed in the Bill of Rights.

Section 5 Summary

A Troubled Past

1 Before independence, Latin America was ruled by European nations. After independence, criollos had political power and caudillos ruled many Latin American countries. Most mestizos and Native
5 Americans remained poor. The lives of former slaves did not get much better after slavery ended.

The caudillos often turned into dictators. They ignored the laws of the new nations. There were revolts and some dictators were overthrown. But many
10 times these dictators were replaced by other caudillos.

Before independence, Spain and Portugal would export farm products and minerals from Latin America. The colonies had to buy goods, or imports, from the countries that ruled them. After independ-
15 ence, they were free to trade with other countries. The United States became an important trading partner.

Foreign companies began to buy large farms and mines in Latin America. They built seaports and railroads to make it easier to take resources out of Latin America. The United States and other foreign nations supported governments that helped these companies.

In 1903, the United States wanted to build a canal across Panama. Panama was part of Colombia. Colombia refused permission. U.S. President Theodore Roosevelt backed a revolt by the people of Panama. Once Panama was independent, it allowed the United States to build the Panama Canal. Now the United States had even more interest in Latin America. In 1904, President Roosevelt claimed that the United States had the right to keep law and order there. He also said the United States could force Latin American nations to pay their foreign debt. ✓

Key Terms

dictator (DIK tay tur) *n.* a ruler with complete power
export (eks PAWRT) *v.* to send products from one country to be sold in another
import (im PAWRT) *v.* to bring products into one country from another
foreign debt (FAR in det) *n.* money owed by one country to other countries

---

⊙ **Target Reading Skill**

Reread the first bracketed paragraph at left. Then read the bracketed paragraph below it to see why the United States became involved in Colombia. If Colombia had given permission for the Panama Canal, do you think there would be a nation of Panama today?

_____

_____

✓ **Reading Check**

What role did President Roosevelt think the United States should have in Latin America?

_____

_____

_____

_____

_____

_____

What happened when Mexico could not pay its debt?

_____

_____

_____

The Struggle Continues

In the mid-1900s, there were still big gaps between the rich and poor in Latin America. Some groups wanted to divide the land more equally. Demand for changes continued into the 1960s and 1970s. During this time, military regimes seized power in many Latin American countries. These regimes ruled harshly. They controlled the press and outlawed political parties. They even killed people who opposed them. By the 1980s, elected governments replaced some of them.

But Latin America's economic problems continued. Many countries had borrowed money. Then, in 1982, the prices of Latin American products fell. Latin

45 American countries had to spend more money for things they needed. As a result, they had to borrow even more money from wealthy countries. Then they found they had to borrow more money just to pay off their debts. When Mexico could not pay its debt, two

50 international organizations stepped in to lend it money. But the money came with strict conditions. ✓

Debt, loss of jobs, more foreign ownership of farms, and cuts to programs for the poor caused many problems in Latin America.

55 Today Latin American countries are working with one another in trade organizations. In 1994, the North American Free Trade Agreement, or NAFTA, came into effect. It made trade easier between Mexico, the United States, and Canada.

Review Questions

1. How did Latin America's economy change after independence?

_____

_____

2. What kinds of problems did Latin American countries face after independence?

_____

_____

Key Term

regime (ruh ZHEEM) *n.* a particular administration or government

1. Mayan civilization thrived in
   A. the Valley of Mexico.
   B. Central America and southern Mexico.
   C. Cuzco, a village in the Andes.
   D. on the shore of Lake Titicaca.

2. Which of the following is true of the Incan empire?
   A. It had its capital at Tenochtitlán.
   B. It stretched along the Pacific coast of South America.
   C. It included the present-day countries of Argentina and Brazil.
   D. It was conquered by the Mayan leader Pachacuti.

3. The Treaty of Tordesillas was signed by
   A. Europe and Asia.
   B. the Aztecs and the Incas.
   C. Cortés and Pizarro.
   D. Spain and Portugal.

4. Latin American independence leaders were inspired by
   A. revolutions in North America and France.
   B. revolutions in Haiti and Mexico.
   C. the Portuguese ruler Dom Pedro.
   D. the conquistadors.

5. NAFTA, the North American Free Trade Agreement, was created to
   A. increase trade among the nations in Latin America.
   B. improve the economies of South American nations.
   C. make trade easier between Canada, Mexico, and the United States.
   D. increase trade between European nations and Mexico.

Short Answer Question

How were the Aztec and Incan civilizations similar?

_____

_____

_____

_____

_____

Prepare to Read

Section 1 The Cultures of Mexico and Central America

Objectives

1. Discover the cultural heritage of the people of Middle America.
2. Find out why many people in this region have been moving away from the countryside.

Target Reading Skill

Identify Causes and Effects When you are reading it is important to know *why* something happened and *what* the result will be. This is called cause and effect. A cause makes something happen. It answers the question *"why."* An effect is what happens. It is the result of the cause. It answers the question *"what."*

While you are reading, you will learn about many events. After you have read a section, stop and ask yourself, "What happened?" Once you have figured that answer out, ask yourself, "Why did this happen?" Putting answers with these questions will help you to understand what you are studying.

In the following example, the cause (*why*) is underlined. The effect (*what*) is marked by a double underline.

Because <u>costs are lower in Mexico,</u> some <u>American companies open factories in Mexico.</u>

Vocabulary Strategy

Word Origins Many words in English come from other languages such as Spanish, German, and French. For instance, did you know that *alligator, patio,* and *cafeteria* are Spanish words? They have been part of the English language for so long that you may not realize they were borrowed from Spanish. In your reading you have already come across some new words that are borrowed from Spanish. They are: *conquistador, hacienda, encomienda, criollo,* and *caudillo.* Spanish words often end with an –*a* or an –*o.* Look for more Spanish words as you read.

Section 1 Summary

1   Middle America is made up of Mexico and the seven nations of Central America. Many people in Middle America are campesinos. Most of them have little or no land of their own. Because of this, it is hard
5 for them to support their families.

Cultural Heritage

Many of the people of Latin America are mestizo. That means they have both Spanish and indigenous ancestors. In Honduras, most of the people are mestizo. The indigenous people of Latin America are also called
10 Native Americans or Indians. In Guatemala most of the people are indigenous. In Costa Rica most of the people are descended from the Spanish. In Belize more than 40 percent of the people have African ancestors.

    Spanish is the main language in most of the coun-
15 tries of Middle America. However, many of the indigenous people speak their own languages, and people in Belize speak English.

    The art of Middle America reflects its history. Before Europeans arrived, Native Americans created many
20 kinds of art. Recent works of art have built on these traditions.

    Religion is important to the people of Middle America. The Spanish settlers were Roman Catholic. Spanish missionaries converted many Native
25 Americans. Today, most of the people are Catholic. However, Native Americans have blended their religions with Christianity.

    Catholic priests and bishops have spoken out against injustice in Middle America. Injustice occurs
30 when people's rights are taken from them. Also, ordinary people have worked to end poverty and injustice by starting health clinics, farms, and organizations. ✓

Key Terms

campesino (kahm peh SEE noh) *n.* a poor Latin American farmer or farm worker

indigenous people (in DIJ uh nus PEA pul) *n.* people who are descended from the people who first lived in a region

---

Vocabulary Strategy

Two new Spanish words are included in this section. Find them in the text and circle them. Write the words and their definitions on the lines below.

_____

_____

_____

_____

✓ Reading Check

Name two ways people have worked to fight poverty and injustice.

1. _____

_____

2. _____

_____

In the bracketed paragraph, there is a cause and effect relationship. Identify the relationship by answering these questions.

What is it that makes it hard for young people to find jobs in the country?

Cause: _____

_____

What is the result of this unemployment?

Effect: _____

_____

Leaving the Countryside

The population of Middle America is growing rapidly. This has made it hard for young people to find jobs in the country. Many have left their homes to look for work in the cities. Today, most people in Middle America live in cities.

In Mexico, some people move to towns near the United States. There, they work in maquiladoras. These are American factories. American companies
40 open factories in Mexico because costs are lower there. Mexican workers assemble parts to make products that will be sent out of Mexico.

Cities in Middle America also offer jobs. As a result, cities have grown quickly. The wealthy people in cities
45 live like wealthy people in the United States. But life in the city can be hard for the poor. There are not enough places to live. It is not easy to find work. It is hard to feed a family on the low wages the poor earn. However, schools are better in cities than in the
50 Mexican country.

Many people in Middle America move to cities if they cannot find work. Thousands of people emigrate to the United States to find jobs. Many immigrants want to return home after earning money to help their
55 families. ✓

Review Questions

1. What are the main languages and religions of the people of Middle America?

_____

_____

2. What is one reason that rural people in Middle America move to cities?

_____

_____

Key Terms

maquiladora (mah kee luh DOHR ah) *n.* a Mexican factory that makes products that will be shipped out of the country
emigrate (EM uh grayt) *v.* to leave one country for another
immigrant (IM uh grunt) *n.* a person who comes into a foreign country to make a new home

---

Prepare to Read

Section 2 The Cultures of the Caribbean

1. Find out what ethnic groups make up the people of the Caribbean.
2. Learn how the different cultures of the region blended to create Caribbean food, music, and celebrations.

Target Reading Skill

Recognize Multiple Causes A cause makes something happen. An effect is what happens. Remember, though, that an effect often can have more than one cause. For example, there is a great variety of foods that are available in the Caribbean. This is an example of an effect that has several causes. One cause is the large variety of seafood that is found there. Another cause is the number of different tropical fruits that grow on the islands. A third cause is the fact that there are so many cultures on the islands. Looking for more than one cause helps you to better understand why something happened. As you read this section, look for other ways that characteristics of Caribbean culture have multiple causes.

Vocabulary Strategy

Word Origins Just as the Caribbean is a blend of cultures, English is a blend of languages. Many words we use every day are borrowed from other languages and cultures. Some of them are borrowed from the Caribbean. Sometimes they have the same meaning. Sometimes they have a different meaning. For example, when you think of the word *carnival*, you probably think of some place that has sideshows, rides, and games. In this section, the word is capitalized because it refers to a specific holiday that is celebrated on many Caribbean islands.

As you read, watch for other words from Caribbean cultures that are also used in American English.

Word Origin	Word	Meaning
Caribbean	Carnival	a holiday that is celebrated on many Caribbean islands

✓ Reading Check

Why are the Caribbean islands sometimes called the West Indies?

_____

_____

_____

⟳ Target Reading Skill

There are very few Native Americans left on the Caribbean islands. Circle the causes of this effect given in the bracketed paragraph.

The People of the Caribbean

When Christopher Columbus arrived in the Caribbean, he thought he had reached the Indies in Asia. He called the people he found Indians. Today, the Caribbean islands are sometimes called the West Indies. There are dozens of different nations in the region, and many peoples and cultures. ✓

The Caribbean gets its name from the Caribs (KA ribz). This group arrived in the area around 1000 A.D. However, they were not the first people on the islands. The Ciboney (SEE boh nay) had lived there for thousands of years. The Arawaks (AH rah wahks) had arrived around 300 B.C. Almost all of these Native Americans were enslaved by the Spaniards. Most of them died of overwork or diseases the Spanish brought with them.

Other Europeans followed the Spanish. In the 1600s, Dutch, French, and English colonists began to claim territory in the Caribbean. European settlers built large sugar plantations and brought African slaves to work on them. Most of the Caribbean people today are descended from the Africans. However, Caribbean ethnic groups include Native American, African, European, Chinese, Indian, and Middle Eastern.

European languages are spoken in the Caribbean. The language of an island depends on the island's history. Languages may be a mixture of European and African languages.

Most West Indians are Christians. There are also small groups of Hindus, Muslims, and Jews. Some people practice traditional African religions.

A Blend of Cultures

Caribbean culture is known for its variety. The people enjoy many kinds of music and dance. They also play a variety of sports. Baseball, soccer, and track and field

---

Key Terms

West Indies (west IN deez) n. the Caribbean islands
ethnic group (ETH nik groop) n. a group of people who share the same ancestry, language, religion, or cultural traditions

are popular. On some islands, people also play cricket.
35 Cricket is a British sport similar to baseball.

Many people in the Caribbean observe Lent, a period of 40 days before Easter. Lent is a very solemn time. Just before Lent begins, a celebration called Carnival is held on most islands. Carnival celebrations 40 include costumes, parades, music and dancing.

Caribbean food uses the region's rich natural resources such as seafood and tropical fruits. People of different cultures enjoy different kinds of food. The table below shows examples.

Country	Food
Barbados	flying fish, sea urchin eggs
West Indies	curry, sausages, Chinese dishes

Caribbean music has both African and European sources. Calypso is a type of song. It uses humorous lyrics and has a distinctive beat. Reggae (REG ay) music comes from Jamaica. Reggae has a strong rhythm. The lyrics often have political messages. Caribbean musicians often use steel drums. The drums are made from recycled oil barrels. Different parts of a steel drum can play different notes ✅.

Vocabulary Strategy

The bracketed paragraph contains two Caribbean words that are used in English. Each word describes a style of music. Circle the words in the paragraph.

✓ Reading Check

Describe two types of Caribbean music.

_____

_____

Review Questions

1. What three groups had settled in the Caribbean before Columbus arrived?

_____

_____

_____

2. Why do West Indians speak a variety of languages today?

_____

_____

_____

Key Term

Carnival (KAHR nuh vul) *n.* an annual celebration just before Lent

Prepare to Read

Section 3 The Cultures of South America

Objectives

1. Find out what ethnic groups are represented in the three cultural regions of South America.
2. Learn what life is like in the countryside and the cities of South America.

Target Reading Skill

Understand Effects A cause makes something happen. The effect is what happens. Sometimes a cause creates more than one effect. You can find this out by answering the question, "What happened?" If there are several answers to that question, the cause had more than one effect. Looking for more than one effect will help you understand fully what took place and will help you to see the connections among the effects.

Read the following paragraph.

<u>The population of South America is booming</u>. There are not enough jobs. City streets are choked with traffic. City governments cannot provide electricity and running water to everyone.

The cause is underlined. Ask yourself the question, "What is happening because of the population boom?" How many effects can you find?

If you can come up with three answers to that question, then you have found the effects!

Vocabulary Strategy

Word Origins English has more "borrowed" words than any other language. These borrowed words have made the English language rich and colorful. They have also made the language very precise. For instance, a gaucho is a cowboy and pampas is a plain. A gaucho, however, is a specific kind of cowboy—one who lives in Argentina. The pampas is a specific plain. It is a plain in Argentina.

When we talk about gauchos on the pampas, we know exactly who they are and where they live. As you read, watch for borrowed words. When you see one, ask yourself "Why is it more precise than the English word would be?"

The People of South America

1 Most of South America was once ruled by Spain. Many South Americans speak Spanish and are Catholic. There are four cultural regions in South America.

The first region is in the north next to the Caribbean 5 Sea. Colombia and Venezuela were Spanish colonies. Their official language is Spanish. Their people are mainly mestizo and Roman Catholic. Guyana was an English colony. Its official language is English. Suriname was a Dutch colony, so its people speak 10 Dutch. In both Guyana and Suriname, many people are Muslim or Hindu. French Guiana is still part of France. Its official language is French. Many of its people are of mixed African and European descent.

The second cultural region is very different from the 15 first. It is made up of Peru, Ecuador, and Bolivia which are Andean countries. Many Native Americans live high in the Andes. Bolivia has more indigenous people than mestizos. The Quechua and Aymará (eye muh RAH) speak their own languages. They follow the tradi- 20 tions of their ancestors.

The third region is made up of Chile, Argentina, Paraguay, and Uruguay. Chile's people are mostly mestizos. Many ethnic groups live in the big cities of Argentina and Uruguay. This region includes the pam- 25 pas, or plains of Argentina. The pampas is the home of Argentinean cowboys called gauchos.

The fourth region is Brazil, the largest country in South America. It was once ruled by Portugal. Its people speak Portuguese. There are many cultures in 30 Brazil. There are Native Americans, and people of African, European, and mixed descent.

Women in South America are fighting for equal rights. They want equality in education, employment, and health care. They also want to have a voice in gov- 35 ernment. ✓

Target Reading Skill

What two effects of Spanish colonization are described in the first paragraph? *Hint:* Ask yourself, "What happened in South America as a result of Spanish rule?"

1. _____

_____

2. _____

_____

✓ Reading Check

What rights are women fighting for?

_____

_____

Key Term

gauchos (GOW chohz) *n.* cowboys of the pampas of Argentina

Country and City Life

South America has cities with huge populations, but it also has large areas where there are almost no people at all.

40 Except in Chile, Argentina, and Uruguay, most rural people who own land do subsistence farming. Very large farms grow crops to export to other countries. The main cash crops of South America are coffee, sugar, cocoa, and bananas. So much land is used for 45 cash crops that South America has to import much of the food for its people to eat.

Spanish colonists founded many of the major cities of South America. The architecture is Spanish in style. Some buildings follow Native American designs. There 50 are also modern office blocks and apartment buildings in many cities. Brasília, the capital of Brazil, is a completely planned city. It was built in the 1950s so that people from the coast would move to the interior. ✓

The population of South America is booming. People cannot find enough jobs in rural areas. They move to cities, and often end up in poor neighborhoods. People are moving into the cities so quickly that the cities find it nearly impossible to provide electricity and water to everyone. Slums have grown up in many South American cities. They are called *favelas* (fuh VE lus) in Brazil and *ranchos* in Venezuela.

Review Questions

1. Describe two kinds of farms in South America.

_____

_____

_____

2. How does the movement of people from the countryside to urban areas put pressure on cities?

_____

_____

_____

✓ Reading Check

What types of buildings are found in South American cities?

_____

_____

_____

Vocabulary Strategy

When you use borrowed words, it is important to be sure that you know their correct meanings. In the bracketed paragraph, the Spanish word *ranchos* is used in a very different way than you are used to seeing it. On the lines below, write the meaning for *ranchos* as it is used in the country of Venezuela.

_____

_____

_____

1. Many citizens of Latin America are
   A. from Africa.
   B. Native Americans.
   C. mestizos.
   D. all of the above.

2. People in Belize speak
   A. Spanish.
   B. English.
   C. Portuguese.
   D. Latin.

3. Many Native Americans died in the Caribbean due to
   A. intermarriage.
   B. modernization.
   C. ethnic diversity.
   D. overwork and disease.

4. Most of South America was once ruled by
   A. Spain.
   B. France.
   C. England.
   D. Italy.

5. The main cash crops of South America include
   A. coffee and sugar.
   B. cotton.
   C. apples and peaches.
   D. avocados and tangerines.

Short Answer Question

What are some of the effects of rapid population growth in Latin America?

_____

_____

_____

_____

_____

Prepare to Read

Section 1 Mexico: Moving to the City

Objectives

1. Learn what life is like for people in rural Mexico.
2. Find out why many Mexicans have been moving from the countryside to the cities.
3. Understand why the growth of Mexico City presents challenges for people and the environment.

Target Reading Skill

Use Context Clues When you come across a word you don't know, you can often figure out its meaning from its context. A word's context is the words, phrases, and sentences that surround it. Sometimes the context will actually include a definition of the word.

Your textbook often states the definitions of new words in the same sentence or surrounding sentences. The definition of the new word is in words you know. As you read your text, watch for stated definitions whenever you see a new word.

In this example, the phrase in italics explains what smog is:

Smog, *a low-lying layer of polluted air*, hung over the city.

In this section, you will read this sentence: *At the center of most villages is a public square called a plaza.* From context, you can figure out that the word *plaza* means *a public square at the center of a village.*

Vocabulary Strategy

Recognizing Signal Words Signal words are words or phrases that give you clues or directions when reading. Sometimes a signal word or phrase will alert you that two or more things are being compared. Here are some words that may signal a comparison.

also	equally	like	same
as did	in the same way	likewise	same as
as well as	just as	more	similar to
both	less	resemble	too

Section 1 Summary

Life in Rural Mexico

1 Most farm families in Mexico are poor. Some grow their own food on small farms. The farmers and their families often do all the work by hand. Some farm workers do not own any land. They are migrant work-
5 ers. They work on large farms owned by rich landown-ers. Migrant workers travel from one area to another, picking crops that are in season.

Mexico's best farmland is in the southern part of the Mexican plateau. Life has changed little there over
10 many years. At the center of most villages is a public square called a plaza. The village market is held in the plaza. When farm families grow more than they need, they sell it at the market. They buy almost everything they need at the market. ✓

Moving to Mexico City

15 Mexico's population is growing quickly. There is not enough farm work for so many people. Many rural people move to the cities because they cannot find work in the countryside. They hope to make a better life for themselves and their children.
20 Many of the poor people who go to Mexico City cannot afford to build sturdy houses when they arrive. They often become squatters. They build temporary houses on land that does not belong to them. Squatter families hope to buy land from the government and
25 build permanent houses.

Even in Mexico City, many families cannot find work. Sometimes the fathers find jobs in the United States. Many of them send money home every month. Children in these families may not see their fathers for
30 months at a time. They may have to work at low-pay-ing jobs to help support their families ✓

Key Terms

migrant worker (MY grunt WUR kur) *n.* a laborer who travels from one area to another, picking crops that are in season

plaza (PLAH zuh) *n.* a public square at the center of a village

squatter (SKWAHT ur) *n.* a person who settles on someone else's land without permission

✓ **Reading Check**

Describe a rural Mexican village.

_____

_____

_____

✓ **Reading Check**

How do poor people live in Mexico City?

_____

_____

_____

Opportunities and Challenges

Mexico City was built on the site of the Aztec capital Tenochtitlán. Now it is the capital of the modern nation of Mexico. In 2000, nearly 20 million people lived in
35 Mexico City. The population continues to grow. It is one of the largest cities in the world.

Mexico City has modern skyscrapers as well as older, historic areas. The streets and highways can barely handle all of the traffic. There are small neighborhoods where very wealthy people live. Most of Mexico City's residents, however, are not rich. The poorest people live in the far outskirts of town. Some of them must travel several hours a day to get to their jobs.

Because of rapid population growth, many of
45 Mexico's large cities face problems. Streets are jammed with vehicles. The air is polluted with exhaust fumes and smoke from factories. The mountains around Mexico City trap the pollution over the city. The city has outgrown its fresh water supply.

50 Still, there are many ways to make a living in the large cities. Millions of people work in factories and offices. Thousands more sell goods from stalls on the streets. Street vendors are an important part of city life.

In 1994, the North American Trade Association, or
55 NAFTA, was signed. NAFTA makes it easier for Canada, the United States, and Mexico to trade with each other. NAFTA has brought both benefits and disadvantages to Mexico.

In 2000, Vicente Fox was elected president of
60 Mexico. Before that, one political party had ruled Mexico for 71 years. Fox ran against the party. He strengthened Mexico's relationship with the United States. ☑

Review Questions

1. Why do so many rural Mexicans move to the cities?

_____

_____

_____

2. What are the causes of pollution in Mexico City?

_____

_____

_____

Vocabulary Strategy

In the bracketed paragraph, circle all words or phrases that signal comparison.

Mark the Text

Target Reading Skill

What is NAFTA? Look for words or phrases that explain what NAFTA is and circle them.

Mark the Text

✓ Reading Check

What changes has Mexico gone through during the past few decades?

_____

_____

_____

Section 2 Guatemala: Descendants of an Ancient People

Objectives

1. Learn why there is a struggle for land in Guatemala.
2. Find out how the Mayas lost their land.
3. Discover how groups are working to improve the lives of Guatemala's indigenous people.

Target Reading Skill

Use Context Clues Context, the words and phrases that surround a word, can help you understand a new word. Sometimes, a word's context contrasts it with a word or words with the opposite meaning. If you know what the opposite means, you can figure out what the new word means.

Contrasts may be direct, using words such as *but* and *however*. Sometimes, contrasts are implied. This means that there is no single clue that a contrast is being made. Here is an example of an implied contrast:

> The struggle of the *indigenous* people of Guatemala to keep their land began when the Spanish *first arrived*.

In this example, the indigenous people of Guatemala are contrasted with the newly arrived Spanish. Because you know that the Spanish are newly arrived, the *indigenous* Guatemalans must be the people who were already there, or native to the area.

Vocabulary Strategy

Recognizing Signal Words Signal words are words or phrases that give you clues or directions when reading. They tell you that what is coming next will be different in some way from what you have just read. Sometimes a signal word or phrase will alert you that there is a contrast. Here are some words that may signal a contrast.

although	however	on the other	yet
but	not	hand	in contrast
		though	

1 Native Americans make up the majority of the population of Guatemala. They form 23 ethnic groups. The largest group is the Quiché Maya. Many Native Americans are very poor and struggle to make a living.

The Struggle for Land

5 Most land in Guatemala belongs to a few rich families. These rich landowners are known as ladinos.

Most Mayas live in the mountains. They live there because for a long time, it was the only land available to Native Americans. It is hard to produce good crops 10 on this land. The soil is poor, and soil erosion makes farming even harder. ✓

Native Americans grow maize, beans, and squash on their small farms. In contrast, the best land is used for haciendas where crops are grown for export.
15 Haciendas grow coffee, cotton, sugar cane, and bananas. Since the 1930s, land reform has been a goal of many reform groups. The wealthy landowners are against reform. Clashes between people for and against reform have led to violence and civil war.

The Mayas Lose Their Land

20 The Mayas of Guatemala have faced many challenges. Native Americans have little political power and own very little. Mayas think of themselves as Mayan rather than Guatemalan. The majority of Native Americans in Guatemala cannot read or write. This is why most 25 Mayas have not filed papers with the government to show that they own their land.

✓ Reading Check

How is land distributed in Guatemala?

_____

_____

_____

⟳ Target Reading Skill

If you do not remember what hacienda means, consider these context clues. A hacienda is "where crops are grown for export." Haciendas are also contrasted with small farms. Therefore, a hacienda is

_____.

Key Terms

ladino (luh DEE noh) n. a mestizo, or person of mixed Spanish and Native American ancestry in Guatemala

land reform (land ree FAWRM) n. the effort to distribute land more equally and fairly

---

Beginning around 1960, a civil war raged in Guatemala for more than 30 years. Thousands of people were killed. In hundreds of villages, soldiers forced the Mayas off their land. Many Mayas lost everything. Some had to leave the country. ☑

Working for a Better Life

Although many Mayas left Guatemala because of the civil war, some did not. Some of the people who stayed started political movements.

These movements work to fight poverty and bring human rights to the Mayas. They help villages plan ways to protect themselves. They teach people the history of their land and how to read. They help organize meetings, protests, and strikes. Most importantly, these political movements defend the land rights of Native Americans. As a result of these efforts, Mayas have gained more of a voice in the government than they used to have. ☑

Agreements were signed to end the civil war in 1996. The government promised to rebuild Mayan villages. However, not all of these agreements have been carried out. Government violations of human rights increased in 2000, setting off new protests.

Review Questions

1. How is land used in Guatemala?

_____

_____

_____

2. What are two reasons the Mayas lost their land?

_____

_____

_____

Key Terms

political movement (puh LIT ih kul MOOV munt) *n.* a large group of people who work together for political change
strike (stryk) *n.* a refusal to work until certain demands of workers are met

Vocabulary Strategy

In the bracketed paragraphs, circle any words or phrases that signal contrast.

✓ **Reading Check**

How do political movements try to help the Mayas?

_____

_____

Prepare to Read

Section 3 Panama: An Important Crossroads

Objectives

1. Find out why people wanted to build a canal across the Isthmus of Panama.
2. Learn how the Panama Canal was built.
3. Understand how the canal has affected the nation of Panama.

Target Reading Skill

Use Context Clues Sometimes as you read, you come across a word you know, but it is being used in a different way. At first the word does not make sense in the sentence. Most words in English have more than one meaning. When this happens, you could look up the word in a dictionary. But you can often use context clues and your own general knowledge to figure out what the word means without having to look it up. Look at this sentence:

Every water <u>vessel</u> was covered with mesh to keep mosquitoes out.

The word *vessel* may seem out of place here. Perhaps you know that the word *vessel* means "ship," and that a cargo ship carries cargo. Therefore, a water vessel is probably a container that carries or holds water.

Vocabulary Strategy

Recognizing Signal Words Signal words are words or phrases that give you clues or directions when reading. They tell you that what is coming next will be different in some way from what you have just read.

Sometimes a signal word or phrase will help you find a cause or effect.

Words that signal causes:	Words that signal effects:
because	as a result
if	so
since	then
on account of	therefore

Why Build a Canal?

1 The Panama Canal is a short-cut across the Isthmus of 5 Panama. It is the only way to get from the Pacific Ocean to the Atlantic Ocean by 10 ship without going all the way around South America. It short-ens the trip by 15 7,800 miles (12,553 kilome-ters), saving time and money.

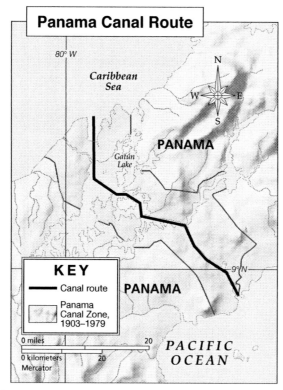

Panama Canal Route

80° W

Caribbean Sea

N

W — E

S

PANAMA

Gatún Lake

KEY

—— Canal route

Panama Canal Zone, 1903–1979

PANAMA

9° N

0 miles 20

0 kilometers 20

Mercator

PACIFIC OCEAN

President Theodore Roosevelt felt that a canal was important for the United States. It would speed trade 20 between the Atlantic and Pacific coasts. It would also allow the U.S. navy to move back and forth in case of war. However, Colombia would not allow the United States to build the canal.

Business people in Panama thought the canal would 25 help the local economy. Also, many Panamanians wanted to be free from Colombia. They saw the canal as a chance for independence. ✓

Because of this, the United States helped Panama revolt against Colombia in November 1903. In return, Panama gave the United States the rights to build the canal.

Key Terms

Panama Canal (PAN uh mah kuh NAL) *n.* a shipping canal across the Isthmus of Panama, linking the Atlantic Ocean to the Pacific Ocean

✓ **Reading Check**

Why did Panamanians want a canal?

_____

_____

_____

Vocabulary Strategy

In the bracketed paragraph, circle any words that signal cause or effect.

Mark Text

You know that standing can mean a person "staying still in an upright position." Look at the underlined sentence. Use what you know about the word *standing* to help you understand what *standing water* means.

_____

_____

_____

✓ Reading Check

How did workers fight the mosquitoes?

_____

_____

_____

✓ Reading Check

Why is the Panama Canal important today?

_____

_____

_____

Building the Canal: A Heroic Effort

Americans had to design and build locks to raise and lower water levels so that ships could move between the oceans. The biggest problem was disease. Malaria 35 and yellow fever killed thousands of workers.

In the 1900s, doctors discovered that mosquitoes spread disease. To kill mosquitoes, workers burned sulfur in every house. <u>Mosquitoes breed in standing water, so swamps were filled with dirt.</u> It took eight 40 years and 70,000 workers to build the Panama Canal. ✅

Panama and Its Canal

The United States and Panama signed a treaty that gave the United States the right to control the canal and the Canal Zone forever.

45 Panama felt that the United States had too much power in their country. In 1977, the United States gave Panama more control over the canal. Panama finally took over the Panama Canal in 1999.

The Panama Canal is very important. It has made 50 Panama a trade, bank, and finance center. ✅

Tourism is also important. Many tourists come to Panama to see the canal. They also visit Panama's rain forests. Panama promotes ecotourism. Ecotourists come to see the rain forest plants and animals.

Review Questions

1. What are the benefits of the Panama Canal?

_____

_____

2. What difficulties did the builders of the canal face?

_____

_____

Key Terms

lock (lahk) *n.* a section of waterway in which ships are raised or lowered by adjusting the water level

Canal Zone (kuh NAL zohn) *n.* a 10-mile strip of land along the Panama Canal, once governed by the United States

ecotourism (ek oh TOOR iz um) *n.* travel to unspoiled areas in order to learn about the environment

1. People who travel from one area to another harvesting crops are known as
   A. squatters.
   B. migrant farm workers.
   C. maquiladoras.
   D. immigrants.

2. The mountains around Mexico City cause it to have problems with
   A. unemployment.
   B. housing.
   C. pollution.
   D. traffic.

3. Most land in Guatemala belongs to
   A. the Quiché Mayas.
   B. Native Americans.
   C. ladinos.
   D. the Guatemalan military.

4. Which country built the Panama Canal?
   A. the United States
   B. France
   C. Panama
   D. Colombia

5. Who controls the Panama Canal today?
   A. the United States
   B. NAFTA
   C. Panama
   D. Colombia

Short Answer Question

How do political movements in Guatemala try to help the Mayas?

_____

_____

_____

_____

_____

Prepare to Read

Section 1 Cuba: Clinging to Communism

Objectives

1. Find out what led Cubans to leave their homeland.
2. Discover how Cuban exiles feel about their lives in the United States and about their homeland.
3. Learn what changes have recently come to Cuba.

Target Reading Skill

Identify Main Ideas It is easier to remember the main idea of a paragraph than every detail. The main idea is the most important point. It is the one that includes all of the details.

Practice finding the main idea using this paragraph.

> Shortly after Cuba gained its independence from Spain, Cuba became rich. In fact, Cuba was the richest country in the Caribbean. Sugar planters made money selling to people in the United States. Hotels and restaurants were built. Tourists came to the island to enjoy the beautiful beaches and warm climate.

To find the main idea, ask yourself, "What is this paragraph about?" The main idea is, Cuba was the richest country in the Caribbean. The rest of the paragraph has the details that tell how Cuba became rich. See if you can find three details that explain how Cuba became rich.

Vocabulary Strategy

Recognizing Roots Often, a few letters are added to the beginning or end of a word to make another word. For example, the letters *un-* may be attached at the beginning of a word. Or the letters *-ing* may be attached at the end of a word. Take away the added letters, and you are left with the root. A root is used to make other words. The word *well* is the root of the word *unwell*. The word *carry* is the root for *carrying*. See how adding letters to the root changes its meaning.

When you come across a new word, look at it closely. See if it contains a root word that you already know.

Section 1 Summary

Cuba's History

Although it is a small island nation, Cuba has many advantages. It has fertile farmland and excellent harbors. In addition, Cuba's location makes it a convenient place for trade.

In 1898, Cuba gained its independence from Spain. With its sugar plantations and tourism, Cuba became the richest country in the Caribbean. Many Cubans became teachers, doctors, and lawyers.

Not all Cubans became wealthy. Farm and factory workers were paid very little. Cuba also had harsh dictators. In 1959, a group led by Fidel Castro overthrew the government. Castro is still in power today. His government is Communist. Castro's government took over all the businesses and land. Anyone who disagreed with Castro was jailed. Many Cubans fled.

Some things improved under communism. Many Cubans were illiterate. Castro sent teachers into the countryside. Today, almost all Cubans can read and write. The government also provides basic health care for all.

Cuba became an ally of the Soviet Union. The Soviet Union was the most powerful Communist country in the world. The Soviet Union wanted to spread communism around the world. The Soviets sent money and supplies to Cuba.

In 1962, the United States discovered that the Soviets were building missile sites in Cuba. President Kennedy demanded that the missiles be removed. His demand caused the Cuban Missile Crisis. The Soviets agreed to remove the missiles if the United States promised not to invade Cuba. ✓

Key Terms

Fidel Castro (fih DEL KAS troh) *n.* Cuba's leader

communism (KAHM yoo niz um) *n.* an economic system in which the government owns businesses and land

illiterate (ih LIT ur ut) *adj.* unable to read and write

ally (AL eye) *n.* a country joined to another country for a special purpose

---

Target Reading Skill

What is the main idea of the first paragraph? Underline the sentence that best states it.

Vocabulary Strategy

Each of the underlined words to the left contains another word that is its root. Circle the roots you find in these words. The root of the first word, "tourism," is "tour."

✓ Reading Check

What was the Cuban Missile Crisis?

_____

_____

_____

Cuban Exiles

After Castro took power, many Cubans began leaving their country. They became exiles. Many Cubans came to the United States. Often they left family members
35 behind. Many exiles dream of returning to Cuba once it is no longer a Communist country.

A large number of exiles have settled in Miami, Florida. In the Cuban neighborhood of Little Havana, they keep their language and culture alive. At the
40 same time, they have become an important part of life in Miami and the state of Florida. ☑

The government of the Soviet Union collapsed in 1991. It could no longer help Cuba. Food, medicines, tools, and other supplies became even scarcer in
45 Cuba. Some families only had rice to eat. As life in Cuba became harder and harder, more people wanted to leave the island.

Changes Come to Cuba

In the 1990s, Castro tried to help Cuba by allowing people to own businesses. The Cuban government
50 began encouraging tourism. At the same time, the United States allowed more people to travel to Cuba. The Cuban economy is improving. Cuban exiles hope that they will be able to visit Cuba again once Fidel Castro is gone. ☑

Review Questions

1. How did Castro come to power in Cuba?

_____

_____

_____

2. What role did the Soviet Union play in Cuba?

_____

_____

_____

Key Term

exile (EK syl) *n.* a person who leaves his or her homeland for another country, often for political reasons

---

✓ **Reading Check**

What is life like for Cuban exiles that live in Miami, Florida?

_____

_____

_____

✓ **Reading Check**

What changes did Castro make in the 1990s?

_____

_____

_____

CHAPTER 15

Prepare to Read

Section 2 Haiti:
A Struggle for Democracy

Objectives

1. Find out how democracy has been threatened in Haiti.
2. Learn what life is like for the people of Haiti, both in the countryside and in the cities.

Target Reading Skill

Identify Supporting Details The main idea of a paragraph or section is the most important point. When you identify the main idea, you know what the paragraph or section is about.

The main idea of a paragraph or section is supported by details. Details give more information about the main idea. They tell you *what, where, when, why, how much,* or *how many.*

Find the section titled "The People of Haiti." In that section the main idea is that the people who live in Haiti share a blend of cultures, and are very poor. As you read, notice the facts that tell you more about how cultures blend in Haiti. Look for details that tell about poverty. You will find facts about culture, ancestry, language, and how Haitians live in the country and the city. These are the details that support the main idea.

Vocabulary Strategy

Finding Roots Often, syllables or groups of syllables are added at the beginning or end of a word to make a new word. The meaning of the new word is related to the original word. But it is changed in some way.

For example, we can add the syllable *un-* at the beginning of *well. Un-* means "not" or "no," so the new word, *unwell,* means the opposite of the word, *well.* It is still related to *well* because it uses *well* as its root.

When you come across a new word, look at it closely. See if it contains any other words that you already know. Then use the new word's root to help you figure out what it means.

Democracy in Danger

1 Haiti's history has been a long struggle for democracy. The struggle has brought violence and economic disaster. The rich in Haiti have fought to keep control of the country. Still, René Préval was <u>democratically</u> elected 5 president in 2006. Many poor people supported him.

The previous president, Jean-Bertrand Aristide, had been forced out of office in 2004. Aristide was first elected president in 1990. Within months, he was forced to leave the country. The military also attacked 10 his supporters. Thousands of Aristide's supporters fled Haiti by sea. They became known as the Haitian boat people. Many of these refugees headed for the United States.

Haiti is on the <u>western</u> third of the island of 15 Hispaniola. It was once a colony of France. Europeans brought Africans to Haiti to work as slaves on sugarcane and coffee <u>plantations</u>. In the 1790s, slaves began to revolt. In 1801, Toussaint L'Ouverture helped end slavery in Haiti.

20 L'Ouverture's goal of <u>freedom</u> and <u>equality</u> was never reached. Most of Haiti's presidents became dictators. One of the worst was François Duvalier (frahn SWAH doo vahl YAY), who took power in 1957. Because he had been a country doctor, Haitians called him 25 "Papa Doc." He was followed by his son, Jean-Claude Duvalier (zhan KLAWD doo vahl YAY), or "Baby Doc." Baby Doc was forced to leave the country. He was replaced with one dictator after another.

Aristide returned to Haiti in 1994. There was a 30 return to democratic <u>government</u>. When Aristide was elected president again in 2000, the election results were challenged. In 2004, rebel groups gained control of much of Haiti, and Aristide left the country once again. ☑

Vocabulary Strategy

Each of the words underlined in the part titled "Democracy in Danger" contains another word that is its root. Circle the roots in these words. The root of the first word, "democratically," is "democrat."

✓ Reading Check

What happened as a result of the 2000 elections?

_____

_____

_____

Key Terms

Jean-Bertrand Aristide (zhan behr TRAHN ah rees TEED) *n.* former president of Haiti

refugee (ref yoo JEE) *n.* someone who leaves his or her homeland to protect personal safety and to escape persecution

---

The People of Haiti

Haitian culture is a blend of African, French, and West Indian cultures. Most of the people are descended from Africans brought as slaves. Haitians who have African and European ancestry are Creole. They are a minority in Haiti. They have most of the wealth and power. Creole is also the name of the language of Haiti. It is based on both French and African languages. ✓

Haiti is the poorest country in the Western Hemisphere. About two thirds of the people try to make a living farming. But the land is overused. Most
45 trees have been cut down. Rain washes the topsoil into the sea. Because farmers cannot feed their families on what they grow, many people have moved to the cities. Poor people live in dirty, crowded neighborhoods with unpaved streets. Meanwhile, the wealthy live in large
50 wooden houses on hills overlooking the city.

Haiti's democracy is once more at risk. The economy has been hurt as well. Most people are still poor. Violence is common. Many want to leave their homeland for a better life. You can see from the chart other
55 problems in Haiti.

Haiti Today

Unemployment	Ratio of Doctors to People	Life Expectancy
70%	1 doctor per 5,000 people	52 years

Review Questions

1. Who are the Haitian boat people?

_____

_____

_____

2. What are the major problems facing Haiti today?

_____

_____

_____

Key Term

Creole (KREE ohl) *n.* a person of mixed African and European descent; in Haiti, a language that mixes French and African languages

Target Reading Skill

What details in this paragraph explain the main idea: Haitian culture blends African, French, and West Indian traditions? Underline them in the text to the left.

Mark the Text

✓ Reading Check

Who are the Creole people of Haiti?

_____

_____

_____

Prepare to Read

Section 3 Puerto Rico: An American Commonwealth

Objectives

1. Understand how the people of Puerto Rico are both American and Puerto Rican.
2. Find out what life is like on the island of Puerto Rico.
3. Learn about the three forms of government Puerto Ricans are considering for their future.

Target Reading Skill

Identify Implied Main Ideas Sometimes the main idea of a paragraph is not stated directly. Instead, all the details in a paragraph or section add up to a main idea. It is up to you to put the details together and identify the main idea. See if you can find the implied main idea in this paragraph:

> Many Puerto Ricans have moved to the United States. Many things are different. Puerto Rico has a warm climate, winters in the United States can be very cold. Cities like New York are much bigger than cities in Puerto Rico. The language in the United States is English. People in Puerto Rico speak Spanish. There is a lot to get used to.

Here is a hint to help you find the main idea: Two countries are being compared. Are they alike? Or are they different?

Vocabulary Strategy

Finding Roots Often, syllables are added at the beginning or end of a word to make a new word. This changes the meaning of the word.

In some cases, the spelling of the root changes. The chart has some examples.

Examples of spelling changes		
craze	crazy	crazily
haste	hasty	hastily
haze	hazy	hazily

Notice how the *e* at the end of each word in the first column becomes a *y* in the word in the second column. Look at the third column. What happens to the *y* from the second column in the word in the third column?

Section 3 Summary

¹ Puerto Rico was once a Spanish colony. When Spain lost the Spanish-American war, it gave Puerto Rico to the United States. The United States has slowly given Puerto Rico more control over its own government. In ⁵ 1951, Puerto Rico adopted its own constitution.

Puerto Rican and American

Puerto Rico is part of the United States. Puerto Ricans are <u>American</u> citizens. However, Puerto Rico is not a state. It is a commonwealth. Puerto Ricans cannot vote in <u>presidential</u> elections. They do not pay U.S. taxes. ¹⁰ They have a representative in the United States Congress, but the <u>representative</u> does not have a vote. Puerto Ricans do serve in the armed forces. ✓

Many Puerto Ricans have moved to the mainland United States. Most settle in cities in the Northeast. ¹⁵ There are many <u>differences</u> between life in Puerto Rico and life on the mainland. Puerto Rico has a warm climate, but winters in Northern cities can be very cold. The language of the mainland is English, while people speak Spanish in Puerto Rico.

Life on the Island

²⁰ Many people travel back and forth between the mainland and Puerto Rico. They live for a while in each place. In the 1950s, many Puerto Ricans moved to the mainland. But since 1965, just as many Puerto Ricans have been returning to the island as were leaving it.

As people travel back and forth, they bring customs and products with them. There are many influences from the United States mainland in Puerto Rico. There is also a strong cultural connection to the Caribbean. Most of the people are a mix of Spanish and African ancestry.

Key Terms

constitution (kahn stuh TOO shun) *n.* a statement of a country's basic laws and values

citizen (SIT uh zun) *n.* a person with certain rights and responsibilities under a particular government

commonwealth (KAHM un welth) *n.* a self-governing political unit that has strong ties to a particular country

---

Puerto Rican cities show influences of Spanish, Caribbean, and U.S. mainland culture. About 75 percent of the people of Puerto Rico live in cities. Many work in factories. Others work in the hotels and restau-
35 rants that attract tourists. The capital, San Juan (san HWAHN), has a large waterfront area known as the Condado (kohn DAH do). The Condado is packed with luxury hotels. Nearby are modern skyscrapers. In the old section of San Juan, there are many Spanish-style
40 buildings. A 450-year-old church that was built by the Spanish still stands. ✓

Seeking a New Direction

Puerto Ricans do not agree on what course their island should take in the future. Currently it is a commonwealth of the United States. American businesses on
45 the island have raised the standard of living. The U.S. government sends millions of dollars to the island every year.

If Puerto Rico became a state, it would be the poorest state in the union. Puerto Ricans would be able to
50 vote in U.S. elections, but they would also have to pay U.S. taxes. For these reasons, Puerto Ricans have voted not to become the 51st state of the United States.

Some people would like to see Puerto Rico become a separate nation. Otherwise, they are afraid
55 that Puerto Ricans will become confused about their identity. They want to make sure that Puerto Ricans keep their Spanish language and culture. They also stress Puerto Rico's connection to other Caribbean nations. ✓

Review Questions

1. What is Puerto Rico's relationship to the United States?

_____

_____

_____

2. What three options are Puerto Ricans considering for their future?

_____

_____

_____

✓ **Reading Check**

Describe San Juan.

_____

_____

_____

✓ **Reading Check**

Why are some people in favor of independence for Puerto Rico?

_____

_____

_____

1. Which of the following best describes Cuba's government?
   A. It is the only Spanish colony in the Caribbean.
   B. It is a commonwealth of the United States.
   C. It has a Communist government.
   D. It is a colony of the Soviet Union.

2. Haiti's road to democracy has been slowed by
   A. a one-crop economy.
   B. dictators.
   C. hurricanes.
   D. the Catholic Church.

3. In 1994, Haiti's government was returned to democracy by
   A. Toussaint L'Ouverture.
   B. François Duvalier.
   C. Jean-Claude Duvalier.
   D. Jean-Bertrand Aristide.

4. Which of the following is a commonwealth of the United States?
   A. Cuba
   B. Haiti
   C. Puerto Rico
   D. Miami

5. Which of the following is true of people in Puerto Rico?
   A. They can vote in presidential elections.
   B. They pay United States taxes.
   C. They have a non-voting representative in Congress.
   D. They cannot serve in the armed forces of the United States.

Short Answer Question

How did life in Cuba change after Castro's takeover?

_____

_____

_____

_____

_____

Section 1 Brazil: Geography Shapes a Nation

Objectives

1. Learn about the geography of Brazil.
2. Discover why the rain forests are important.
3. Find out what groups make up the people of Brazil and how they live.

Target Reading Skill

Compare and Contrast When you compare, you look at how things are the same. For example, people in two different countries may speak the same language or follow the same religion. Two countries may have the same geography.

When you contrast, you look at how things are not the same. The climate in one region may be different from the climate in another region. For example, one climate may be tropical and another climate very dry. Because of climate differences, the crops grown in one region may be very different from crops grown in another region.

As you read this section, look for similarities and differences in the geographic regions and cultures of Brazil.

Vocabulary Strategy

Using Prefixes and Roots A prefix attaches to the beginning of a word to make a new word. The word that it attaches to is the root. When a prefix is added to a root, the new word has a different meaning.

Some common prefixes are listed below.

Prefix	Meaning	Example
de	away from, off	descend
in, im	into, within, on, toward	inject, immigrate
re	again	reread
sur	over, upon, above, beyond	surround

Section 1 Summary

¹ In Brazil's rain forest, it is hard for light to get through the canopy formed by treetops. Few people live in the Amazon rain forest. This rain forest, however, is very important to the people of Brazil and to ⁵ people worldwide.

The Geography of Brazil

Brazil's rain forests take up about half the country. In the southeast, there are mountain ranges and river valleys. There are many harbors along the coast. Rio de Janeiro grew up around a harbor. Most of Brazil's ¹⁰ people live near the coast.

The Brazilian government wanted to develop the land away from the coast. In 1957, to attract people to that area, the government started building a new capital, Brasília. They chose a site on the savanna. Today, ¹⁵ almost 2 million people live there. ☑

The Importance of the Rain Forest

The rain forest is important to life all over the world. Rain forests produce oxygen. The Amazon rain forest has several million different types of plants, animals, and insects. Many medicines are made from plants ²⁰ that grow only in the rain forest.

In the past, Brazil gave land in the rain forest to campesinos. They cleared land for their crops. Within a few years, the soil was poor. Logging, mining, and road building also damaged the rain forest. Today, ²⁵ Brazil's leaders are trying to to protect the fragile rain forest from further damage.

✓ Reading Check

Why was Brasília built?

_____

_____

_____

Key Terms

canopy (KAN uh pea) *n.* the dense mass of leaves and branches that form the top layer of a rain forest

Amazon rain forest (AM uh zahn rayn FAWR ist) *n.* a large tropical rain forest in northern South America

Rio de Janeiro (REE oh day zhuh NEHR oh) *n.* a large city in Brazil

Brasília (bruh ZIL yuh) *n.* Brazil's new capital city

savanna (suh VAN uh) *n.* a flat grassy region, or plain

Describe three dangers that threaten the rain forest.

_____

_____

_____

Compare the way the native people lived before the development of the rain forest with the way they live now.

_____

_____

_____

✓ Reading Check

What is Rio de Janeiro like?

_____

_____

_____

There are other dangers to the rain forest. The Brazilian government is trying to stop smuggling of endangered animals and wood. It is trying to stop 30 pollution caused by mining. ✓

Before development, many of the native peoples of the rain forest were isolated. They continued their ancient ways of living. When the rain forest was opened to development, miners, farmers, and land 35 speculators arrived. These people brought new diseases that killed many native people. More were killed in conflicts with developers. The culture of these native peoples began to change.

The People of Brazil

The Native Americans living in the rain forest were 40 some of the first people to live in Brazil. Many Native Americans still live in the rain forest. However, some have left the rain forest for the cities.

Today, most Brazilians are a mix of Native American, African, and European heritages. There are 45 many features of African culture in Brazil. The city of Salvador is like a town in Africa. Some Brazilians are descended from Portuguese colonists. More recently, immigrants have come from Italy and Japan.

In Brazil, a few people own most of the land suitable for growing crops. In the 1990s, the government gave some of this land to poor farmers.

Like many Brazilian cities, Rio de Janeiro is home to the rich and the very poor. It is on the coast, surrounded by mountains. There are expensive hotels 55 and shops for tourists. On the slopes of the mountains, neighborhoods are crowded and dirty. About 20 percent of Rio's people live in homes with no electricity or running water. ✓

Review Questions

1. What are the main features of Brazil's geography?

_____

_____

2. Why are Brazil's rain forests important to the whole world?

_____

_____

Prepare to Read

Section 2 Peru: An Ancient Land Looks to the Future

Objectives

1. Learn how geography has affected the way people live in the three regions of Peru.
2. Discover what life is like in the cities and towns of the Altiplano.

 Target Reading Skill

Identify Contrasts When you contrast, you look at the differences between two things or events. When you read, contrasting will help you see and understand differences. It will also help you understand why things are different. Contrasting is a way of sorting out or figuring out what you read.

Sometimes the contrasting information is all in a single sentence or paragraph. Sometimes it is in more than one paragraph under a single heading. Contrasts may be signaled by words or phrases such as *although, yet, as opposed to, however,* or *on the other hand.*

In this section, you will read about the three geographic regions of Peru. As you read, list what is different about each region.

Vocabulary Strategy

Using Roots and Suffixes A suffix attaches to the end of a word to make a new word. The word it attaches to is the root. When a suffix is added to a root, the word takes on a new meaning.

Some common suffixes are listed below.

Suffix	Meaning	Example
al	of, or like	coastal
fy	to make to cause to have or feel	liquefy putrefy
ic	like, or having to do with	angelic
less	without	treeless

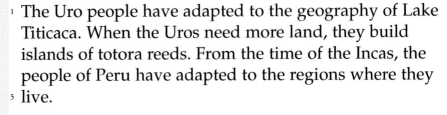

Vocabulary Strategy

The words listed below appear in this section. Each of these words contains a suffix. Underline the suffix in each word. As you do so, think about what each suffix means.

geographic

coastal

economic

treeless

As you read this section, circle the words. Did knowing what the suffix meant help you understand the meaning of each word?

¹ The Uro people have adapted to the geography of Lake Titicaca. When the Uros need more land, they build islands of totora reeds. From the time of the Incas, the people of Peru have adapted to the regions where they ⁵ live.

The Regions and People of Peru

The Andes Mountains run from northwest to southeast Peru. They divide the country into three geographic regions. The sierra region includes the Andes and the Altiplano, a high plateau in the Andes. People have ¹⁰ lived in this region for hundreds of years. The Incas built their empire in the Altiplano. The city of ¹⁵ Cuzco was their capital. Today, the descendants of the Incas live the same way their ancestors ²⁰ lived. They farm and herd sheep, cattle, llamas, and alpacas.

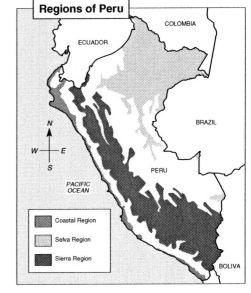

The coastal region is dry. It is dotted ²⁵ with oases where people have lived since before the Europeans arrived. This area is the economic center of Peru. Over one quarter of Peru's population lives in Lima (LEE muh), the capital.

³⁰ The third region of Peru is a large forested area. It stretches from the mountains to the lowlands of northeast Peru. This region is called the selva. The selva has few roads to connect it to the sierra and the coast. Little development has taken place in this region.

Key Terms

sierra (see EHR uh) *n.* the mountain region of Peru
Altiplano (al tih PLAH noh) *n.* a high plateau in the Andes Mountains
oasis (oh AY sis) *n.* a fertile area in a desert that has a source of water (plural: *oases*)

---

35 Native Americans make up more than half of Peru's population. Many of them remain cut off from the modern world. Most of Peru's Native Americans are Quechua. Another 32 percent of the people are mestizo. The remaining Peruvians are of European, African, 40 and Asian ancestry. ✓

Life in the Altiplano

Many of the Native Americans living on the Altiplano follow traditions that are hundreds of years old. However, their communities are slowly changing. Thousands of Native Americans have left for jobs in 45 the city, and life is changing for those who stay in their villages.

The past is easily seen in the Altiplano. There are ruins of Incan cities in the countryside. Most of those who live in cities have electricity. Streets are paved, and there are telephones. In Cuzco, parts of the old Incan city wall are still standing. Modern houses are built on foundations that are the remains of Incan stonework. There are also old buildings.

Village life is very different from city life. In the remote villages, there are no telephones. There are few buses. Most of the people are Quechua or Aymara. The land is treeless tundra.

Like the Uros of Lake Titicaca, the people who live on the tundra have adjusted to their environment. The Quechua raise sheep, animals that are suited to the tundra. The Quechua find time to play soccer. In their schools, they learn about the world around them. ✓

Review Questions

1. What are the three regions of Peru and what are they like?

_____

_____

_____

2. What is Cuzco like?

_____

_____

_____

✓ **Reading Check**

Which two groups make up the majority of Peru's population?

1. _____

2. _____

🎯 **Target Reading Skill**

What contrasts do you see in the bracketed paragraphs between city life and life in an isolated village in the Altiplano?

_____

_____

_____

✓ **Reading Check**

Explain how one group of Peruvians has adapted to their environment.

_____

_____

_____

Prepare to Read

Section 3 Chile: Land of Contrasts

Objectives

1. Find out how the geography of Chile creates regions where people live very differently.
2. Learn how Chile's people live and what products they produce.
3. Find out how Chile restored democracy.

Target Reading Skill

Compare and Contrast When you compare, you examine how things are the same or similar. Similarities are things that are like other things. For example, Chile and Brazil have many similarities. They are both Latin American countries. They are both in South America.

When you contrast, you look at the way things are different. While there are many similarities between Chile and Brazil, there are also many differences. Chile was colonized by Spain, and the main language is Spanish. Brazil was colonized by Portugal, and the main language is Portuguese. Chile is on the Pacific coast of South America. Brazil is on the Atlantic coast.

Putting facts into a Venn diagram is a helpful way to compare and contrast. You could practice by using the information in this skill.

Vocabulary Strategy

Recognizing Compound Words Sometimes when you come across a new word, you can figure out what it means if you break it down into parts. For example, if you did not know what the word *snowball* means, you could break it down into its parts: *snow* and *ball*. A snowball is a ball of snow. Many words in English are made by combining two or more words. Such words are referred to as compound words.

Here are some common words that are made up of two words:

anybody	*homeland*	*seashore*
baseball	*landform*	*skyscraper*
countryside	*mainland*	*southwest*
downtown	*mountaintop*	*waterway*
farmland	*northeast*	*worldwide*

Can you think of any other words that combine two words?

Section 3 Summary

1 In 1520, Ferdinand Magellan found a way through the islands at the "bottom" of South America. The passage he found is in present-day Chile. This passageway allowed sailors from Europe to explore the western
5 coast of South America.

The Geography of Chile

The passage that Magellan discovered is called the Strait of Magellan. It is dangerous to sail through. However it is safer than going around Cape Horn to the south. Magellan's group became the first to circum-
10 navigate the globe. Magellan died during the trip. Only one of the five ships made it back to Spain.

Chile is the longest, narrowest country in the world. It averages only about 100 miles (161 kilometers) wide. But it runs 2,650 miles (4,265 kilometers) down the
15 Pacific coast to the very tip of South America. The Andes Mountains run down the whole length of Chile.

Chile contains different landforms and climates. The Atacama Desert is in the north. The desert is rich in copper. It is a region dotted with mines. Chile exports
20 more copper than any other country in the world.

Chile has a long central valley. There are rolling hills, high grasses, and forests. Most of Chile's people live here. It is also where the capital, Santiago, is located. Farming and mining are important. The beautiful
25 Lakes Region has forests, waterfalls, and volcanic mountains topped by glaciers. ✓

The southern third of Chile is cold, wet, and often stormy. This region is near Antarctica. It has icebergs and penguins.

Key Terms

Ferdinand Magellan (FUR duh nand muh JEL un) *n.* Portuguese explorer whose expedition first circumnavigated the globe

circumnavigate (sur kum NAV ih gayt) *v.* to sail or fly all the way around something, such as Earth

glacier (GLAY shur) *n.* a slow-moving mass of ice and snow

Chile's People and Products

30 The lifestyles of Chileans vary from region to region. In the south, people herd sheep. Many farmers live in the central valley. City people rush around. Mestizos make up more than 90 percent of the population. Only 10 percent of the people are Native Americans. More than 35 80 percent of all people live in cities.

Chile's economy depended heavily on sales of copper. In the 1980s, copper prices fell, which was bad for the economy. Farming became a huge industry. Chile now ships fruits and vegetables around the world.

40 Chile's farming regions are protected by the Andes Mountains. Many insect pests and animal diseases that harm other countries never reach Chile. Therefore, Chilean crops are free of many common plant pests. ✓

Restoring Democracy

In 1973, the armed forces took control of the government 45 of Chile. The military force was led by General Augusto Pinochet Ugarte. He became a brutal dictator.

There were national days of protest. The Catholic Church spoke out against him. In 1988 elections, Pinochet's name was the only one on the ballet. But the 50 people of Chile rejected him by voting "no." Democratic government returned. ✓

Review Questions

1. Describe Chile's geographic regions.

_____

_____

_____

2. Describe life in Chile when Pinochet was in power.

_____

_____

_____

Key Term

Augusto Pinochet Ugarte (ah GOO stow pea noh SHAY oo gahr TAY) *n.* military dictator of Chile from 1973 to 1988

✓ **Reading Check**

Why is Chilean produce free of many plant pests?

_____

_____

_____

✓ **Reading Check**

How did Pinochet's rule end?

_____

_____

_____

CHAPTER 16

Objectives

1. Find out how Venezuela was made wealthy by oil.
2. Learn how the ups and downs of oil prices affected the economy and people of Venezuela.
3. Understand how Venezuela is changing.

Target Reading Skill

Make Comparisons One way to figure out new facts is by comparing them with facts you already know. For example, which of the following facts is easier to understand?

   A. Venezuela has a total area of 340,560 square miles (882,050 square kilometers).

   B. Venezuela is slightly more than twice as large as California.

Most people would choose B.

   As you read this section, compare life in Venezuela to life here in the United States. Be sure to look at facts about the economy, the government, and the people's lives.

Vocabulary Strategy

Using Word Parts Sometimes when you come across a new word, you can figure out what it means if you break it down into smaller pieces or word parts. Look for the root. What does the prefix or suffix mean? Take the meanings of the root and prefix or suffix and add them together. Then you will have found the meaning of the new word.

   Review the tables of prefixes and suffixes that were in other sections of the chapter. The suffix *-ed* indicates an action completed in the past. The suffix *-ing* indicates an action that continues over a period of time.

A Land Made Wealthy by Oil

1 Venezuela has the largest oil reserves in the world after the Persian Gulf region. Venezuelan oil has earned millions of dollars on the world market. Both the government and private corporations own oil companies. In
5 the early 1980s, Venezuela was the richest country in Latin America. Much of the money went to the capital, Caracas. It is also the business center of the country.

During the 1970s, oil prices went up. An oil boom began. The government started to spend a lot of
10 money. People were hired to run government agencies. Subways and roads were built. The government borrowed money so that it could spend even more. The country depended upon the money it got from oil sales to pay back these loans.
15 From the mid-1980s through the 1990s, more oil was produced in the world than was needed. The price of oil started to fall. The government was spending more than it could earn. Many people lost their jobs.

However, oil prices began to rise in the early twen-
20 ty-first century after many Venezuelan oil workers went on strike. By 2004, prices reached their highest point in 20 years. In 2005, they continued to soar. The poverty rate began to go down, but poverty remains a problem in Venezuela. ✓

The Economy and the People

25 Before the oil boom, Venezuela's culture and economy had been based on agriculture. Because of the oil boom, it became a modern country. About 80 percent of the population now lives in cities.

When oil prices fell, many workers lost their jobs.
30 To deal with this problem, the Venezuelan government started a policy of privatization. In the late 1980s and

---

Key Terms

Caracas (kuh RAH kus) *n.* the capital of Venezuela
boom (boom) *n.* a period of business growth and prosperity
privatization (pry vuh tih ZAY shun) *n.* the government's sale of land or industries it owns to private businesses or individuals

the 1990s, the government sold some of its businesses to big companies. It hoped these companies would make big profits and hire more workers. However, the
35 salaries they paid were less than the government had paid. ✅

The economic crisis was made worse by natural disaster. In 1999, huge floods and mudslides hit Venezuela. Many people were killed or left homeless.
40 Reconstruction went on for years.

A Change in Government

In 1998, Hugo Chavez was elected president of Venezuela. He promised to help the poor. However, some people challenged Chavez. In 2002, he was briefly forced out of office during an attempted coup.
45 He also faced protests and a strike that halted oil production. Most voters, though, still supported him.

Chavez started many new programs. He used money from oil sales to give poor people basic services. However, Chavez's critics disagreed with many of his
50 policies. Some of these policies hurt the relationship between Venezuela and the United States. ✅

Venezuela's economy has improved in recent years. Oil prices have risen. Fewer people are unemployed and live in poverty. These improvements may help
55 Chavez win reelection.

Review Questions

1. How did the government of Venezuela react to the oil boom?

_____

_____

_____

2. Why did the drop in oil prices affect Venezuela so much?

_____

_____

_____

Key Term

coup (koo) *n.* the overthrow of a ruler or government by an organized group which then takes power

How did salaries for many workers compare before and after privatization?

_____

_____

_____

Vocabulary Strategy

The words below appear in the part titled "A Change in Government." Each of these words contains either a prefix or a suffix. Two words contain both.
Underline the prefix or suffix in each word. As you do so, think about how each prefix and suffix changes the meaning of the root.

elected	unemployed
promised	reelection
disagreed	

✓ **Reading Check**

How did Hugo Chavez gain support from the poor?

_____

_____

_____

1. Brazil's most valuable and fragile resource is its
   A. rain forests.
   B. coffee plantations.
   C. favelas.
   D. factories.

2. Peru's economic center is in the
   A. sierra.
   B. Altiplano.
   C. coastal region.
   D. selva.

3. Chile needed to find other ways to make money when the price on the world market fell for
   A. oil.
   B. copper.
   C. coffee.
   D. consumer goods.

4. The government's sale of land or industries to private businesses is
   A. diversification.
   B. nationalization.
   C. privatization.
   D. democratization.

5. Why did Venezuela's oil industry suffer from the mid 1980s through the 1990s?
   A. The oil fields began to dry up.
   B. People weren't driving cars as much.
   C. The country started to focus on agriculture.
   D. World oil prices fell.

Short Answer Question

What happened when the native people of Brazil's rain forests came into contact with the outside world?

_____

_____

_____

_____

_____